Contemporary
Cube Bead Designs

Stitching with Herringbone, Peyote, Ladder Stitch, and more

VIRGINIA JENSEN

KALMBACH BOOKS

Kalmbach Books
21027 Crossroads Circle
Waukesha, Wisconsin 53186
www.Kalmbach.com/Books

Published in 2012

16 15 14 13 12   1 2 3 4 5

Manufactured in the United States of America

ISBN: 978-0-87116-436-0

Editor: Erica Swanson
Technical Editor: Stacy Werkheiser
Art Director: Lisa Bergman
Graphic Designer: Rebecca Markstein
Photographer: James Forbes

Library of Congress Cataloging-in-Publication Data
Jensen, Virginia, 1941-
   Contemporary cube bead designs : stitching with herringbone, peyote, ladder stitch, and more / Virginia Jensen.

      p. : ill. (some col.) ; cm.

   ISBN: 978-0-87116-436-0

   1. Jewelry--Design. 2. Jewelry making--Handbooks, manuals, etc. 3. Beadwork--Patterns. 4. Beadwork--Handbooks, manuals, etc. 5. Decoration and ornament--Handbooks, manuals, etc. I. Title.

TT212 .J46 2012
739.27

Contents

Introduction

HOW I CAME TO WRITE ANOTHER BOOK

After publication of the first cube bead book, *Cube Bead Stitching,* my editor asked if I had enough work for a second book. I had found that even as I was working on the first book, I was still coming up with new ideas, and often had to set aside a new idea in order to get on with my writing. So I picked up those concepts, expanded on them, developed a few more, and there was a second book! Writing the first beadwork book was such a thrill, and there was such a great response to it, I just had to do it again.

STRUCTURE OF THIS BOOK

I've arranged this book differently from the first. In *Cube Bead Stitching*, the pieces are arranged according to the type of piece you make—such as earrings or bracelets. But this time, I thought it would be interesting to give beaders an opportunity to study a particular stitch in depth. I've arranged these designs so that you can learn a stitch (if you don't already know it) and then try various techniques with that same stitch.

This is often the way I work. I will get into a stitch and do nothing but that stitch for a while, experimenting with technique and trying new colors and bead types just to see what they will do. Often it's while I am in this process that creative ideas come to me. Perhaps this will spark a new project for you too!

ABOUT THE ILLUSTRATIONS

Many of us may work better with visual directions. Some people who work with their hands are often not very "mental" and a stream of words can boggle the intellect. But a picture, as they say, is worth a thousand words.

The illustrations I've made for this book are what you would call "exploded" illustrations. The beads are shown spread apart so that you can see how the thread passes between them. Of course, you will pull your beads together as you go.

I've colored the thread paths in a certain order, so that you go from red to blue to orange to purple to green. This is the order in most of the illustrations, unless there is some color conflict. With each new illustration, the colors start over again. Each new color starts with a dot to show where the new action begins, and each color is coordinated with the steps in the written instructions. In addition, I've grayed out the work that is already finished, so the darker beads and thread are the new ones.

I hope these illustrations are so clear that some of you can make the pieces without reading the written instructions at all. Either way, enjoy the designs and have fun creating beautiful, stylish jewelry!

–Virginia

Cube Beads & Other Supplies

ABOUT CUBE BEADS

The primary material in this book is cube beads. There is quite a lot to know about these relatively new products. Many retailers are just beginning to get the full line of cube beads and to realize the potential for beadwork designs.

To purchase any kind of cube bead, the fastest way is to search online; for example, search for "buy 3mm cube beads." I include the word "buy" at the beginning because this eliminates any news or articles about 3mm cubes beads and takes me straight to the vendors. You will find any online dealer who sells these, and there are quite a few. But I also want to encourage everyone to visit their local stores and ask them to carry cube beads. This is the best way to ensure that they will be available in the future. Also check the list of resources at the end of this book.

The two manufacturers of cube seed beads, Toho and Miyuki, are both Japanese companies. Toho refers to its beads as cubes, and Miyuki refers to its beads as squares. In this book, I've used the word cube to refer to either of these beads. I use beads from both sources.

You can distinguish these two manufacturers' beads by looking at them. Toho beads have a square hole and slightly rounded corners along the linear edges; Miyuki beads have a round hole with sharper edges and corners.

The Miyuki line includes square beads in sizes called 1.8mm, 3mm, and 4mm (sometimes called 3.5 or 3.8). The Toho line includes cube beads in sizes called 1.5mm, 2mm, 3mm, and 4mm. These are all in the "seed bead" category and can be found in the seed bead section of catalogs and online stores.

BUYING CUBE SEED BEADS

Unfortunately, buying cubes is kind of like buying a lumber store 2 x 4, which doesn't actually measure 2 in. by 4 in. The millimeter measurement is just a standard used to ensure that you buy the same product every time. This is true with both cube manufacturers.

In working with these beads, I follow my practical experience. There is very little difference between the Miyuki 1.8mm square and the Toho 1.5mm cube. I use them interchangeably. So far, no bead made by Miyuki is the same size as the Toho 2mm cube.

You will also find a bit of variability in the sizes of all the cubes because the manufacturing process creates differences. For example, beads that are tumbled or acid-washed decrease slightly in size, and beads that are coated increase slightly in size.

Sometimes cubes sold as 3.5mm are really 4mm. Check carefully, asking questions wherever possible, or buy a sample before committing to a big purchase.

Cube Beads & Other Supplies

OTHER KINDS OF CUBES

Other kinds of cubes are available. I've used some of them in my designs. One of the cubes I've used is a glass cube with beveled edges made by manufacturers of crystal beads. The smallest I've been able to find is 4mm, but these will work wherever you need a 4mm size and can be combined with the cube seed beads. They are also usually available in 6mm and 8mm.

Another type of square bead is metal. Some vendors carry a hollow metal bead, usually sterling silver. These have rounded corners and usually come in 2mm, 3mm, and 4mm sizes. In actuality, these beads are smaller than that, so I would suggest buying a few to see how they work before committing to an expensive purchase in the wrong size. I used 2mm sterling cubes in combination with the Toho 1.5mm cubes, and they worked just great.

You can sometimes find gem or mineral beads in square shapes. These can be used if they fit, but be sure the holes are large enough to accommodate the number of thread passes.

Another type of cube is called a "square-cut Delica." They are almost indistinguishable from the 1.5mm or 1.8mm cubes. I noticed that the square-cut Delicas I bought seemed more regular in shape with less distortion at the cut end. Try them and see what you think.

WORKING WITH CUBE BEADS

If you are a long-time beader, you may find working with the new cube beads strange. They can create a piece that's uncommonly rigid. The flat sides will lock together and the corners will just get in the way! But if you are a beginner, you may find that the flat sides and large holes make learning quite a bit easier. You can hold them in place better, they don't roll around, and the holes are big enough to see and to pass through easily.

Sharp edges

Because most seed beads are round, they get tumbled to take off any sharp edges. Cube beads need to retain their edges and corners, so they don't always get the same treatment. The beads most likely to have sharp edges are uncoated and matte finish beads. And if you see a bit of glass stuck near the center of the bead or clogging the hole, do not think, "I'll just pop that out." Whenever you break off a piece of any glass bead, you leave a razor-sharp edge that will cut through your thread. Discard that bead.

TOOLS AND OTHER NECESSITIES

You only need a few supplies to begin beading. Here are my favorites:
- #10 beading needle
- 8 lb.- or 10 lb.-test synthetic braided microfilament thread, such as Power Pro
- sharp, small crafters scissors
- super-glue gel
- shallow, small bowls to put beads in (sauce dipping bowls or watercolor mixing bowls)
- magnifying glasses

A note about thread

My favorite thread is a synthetic braided microfilament sold under trade names of Power Pro and Stren, although other brands may be found on the market. This thread is really strong, and is available in many strengths from 5- to 100-lb. test, so I never need a doubled thread. I use mainly 8- and 10-lb. test, though I can pass up to 15-pound through my #10 needle.

Despite its strength, it is fine and flexible, easy to tie, and holds a knot very well. It doesn't stretch, so I don't have to prestretch. Its braiding makes it rounder and harder to split, which is not the case with parallel fiber threads like Nymo. I don't find any kind of conditioner necessary, and I dislike the tacky wax products that stick to the beads as well as the thread.

Even though this is the thread used to make bulletproof vests, it is not impervious; it can be cut with the sharp edge of a broken bead. I defy anyone to break it with their hands. Treat it with respect, and it will serve you very well.

In fact, the only problem I have with this thread is the limited range of colors. However, I love it so much that I will make do with the colors available. The material is so inert that it will not take a dye and has to be coated to acquire color. You can find white, moss green, yellow, red, and blue, but you will have to locate a sporting goods store online to get all these colors.

If I must use another thread, I settle for Fireline, although I find it kinky. Any of the parallel fiber threads are my third choice. I use them only if I need an exact color match.

ADDING THREAD

In my designs, I've tried wherever possible to give you enough thread to finish a piece. When it is necessary to tie on more thread, work the ending thread back and forth through the previous work until it is fairly secure and won't loosen easily. End

Stitch Basics

that thread where you intend to tie off, leaving at least a 6-in. tail. Start a new thread, leaving from where the ending thread came out (That way, the two ends are together) and wend your way back to where you stopped working. I often leave the tails loose until I've finished a piece, and then I go back and end them all at once.

ENDING THREAD

If you've added thread according to my way (see above) you can just tie a surgeon's knot and pull that knot into the adjacent bead to hide it completely. Run the tails out an inch or so from the knot. Tie a half-hitch onto a cross thread—a thread that is crossing the direction you're coming from and going—a few beads before you exit in order to keep the tail from popping out.

Generally, I work two tails together and tie off as above. If I don't have another tail to tie to, I try to get in at least three half-hitches or a couple of double half-hitches on my way out. I try to tie my hitches to a cross thread; otherwise, the knot could slide along the parallel thread and doesn't really knot. Pull these knots gently so they tighten where you want them to.

Because the holes in cube beads are larger than most beads—and the larger the bead, the larger the hole—you will need to tie off with at least one full knot. Running the thread back and forth through the work is just not adequate for these big-holed beads. Only if you are working with 1.5mm cubes and your work is dense, such as peyote or square stitch, can you get away with this.

KNOTS

Half-hitch knot

Form a loop with the thread. Take the needle under a cross thread in the work up, and back through the loop you made. Pull slowly to be sure you have actually tied a knot and not just wrapped the thread.

You can do this again to double the knot; if you went forward under the cross thread the first time, go backward under the same thread and through the loop.

Square knot

There is more than one way to describe this knot; here's my version. Pull the right thread to the right in your right hand, and the left thread to the left in your left hand. Cross the threads in the middle, and take the right thread over, behind, and under the

left thread and back toward you; catch the wrapping (right) thread with your left hand and the other thread with your right hand and pull through to tighten. Pull the threads part again and repeat from the opposite side: Cross the left thread over and under the right thread, change hands, and pull through.

If you get confused about which thread is which, put a needle on the right thread only. You will always be wrapping with the needle. Practice with a cord or larger thread if you need to.

Surgeon's knot

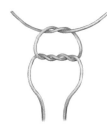

A surgeon's knot is like square knot except that you wrap the first wrap twice, taking the right thread over, behind, under, and forward twice, then pull through to tighten. The wrap from the left is just once, the same as the square knot.

Lark's head (price tag) knot

Fold a thread to form a loop end; put the loop through anything, such as a jump ring, put the tails through the loop and pull them through. Be careful not to let the loop spring back around the jump ring; I like to hold the jump ring with a pair of chainnose pliers.

You can also make this knot another way. Put the loop through a jump ring far enough that you encompass the jump ring, then reach through with your fingers or a pair of pliers and pull the jump ring through the loop. Draw the threads up against the bottom of the jump ring.

ABOUT THE STITCHES

Most beaders are familiar with herringbone, peyote, ladder, and brick. These stitches are all used to make pieces with cube beads. In effect, I've done the work for you of trying out these stitches using cubes to see how they work together. Some work better than others.

As you'll see in this book, I have long chapters on herringbone and step stitch, a stitch I developed from St. Petersburg chain. These two stitches are especially suited to cube beads. Occasionally, I've found a trick that makes one of the other stitches work. A prime example of this is the peyote three-cube cuff. Peyote usually makes a stiff piece, but the combination of the different sizes of cubes creates enough play that the cuff moves freely instead of locking up.

Jewelry Projects

Ladder Stitch

When you make a ladder with cube beads, the sides lock together to form a solid join. You can use this to your advantage to make a base on which other beads of different shapes can be attached. The easiest application for this is to make a ladder and use it as you would a finding called a spacer bar. The tiered bracelet in this chapter does that with panache. Once you get the hang of the bracelet, try making a necklace with the same technique and learn how to add rows to succeeding tiers.

As I began thinking about what else I could do with ladder stitch and cube beads, I realized that the ladder could be folded back on itself, and soon I had a nine-bead square of ladder stitch. It seemed like a great foundation for something, but what to put on it?

The solid, plain square seemed to need balancing with something glittery, and I decided on crystals. Of course they should go at the corners, and of course they should be mirrored again on the bottom to create two pyramid shapes. Soon I had my Chandelier Earrings, p. 18, but they called out for even more. Fringe! I attached long dangles to the bottom sections for an even more exciting chandelier.

The last creation was the Aztec Ladder Bracelet, p. 16. That one came to me in that soft half-dream state early in the morning when I woke. Unlike many of my a.m. imaginings, this one worked out perfectly the first time through.

If you're a beginner, try a couple of these designs first and you will be ready to move on to simple foundation ladders.

YOU'LL NEED:

- 80–90 3mm cube beads in two matching colors
- 25–35 2mm cubes
- 4g 8º seed beads in color A
- 4g 8ºs in color B
- 3-strand clasp
- #10 needle
- 3–4 yd. thread

Tiered Bracelet

This is a fun piece with so much potential! Between the ladders of gold cubes, add different shapes of red and gold beads. A simple design with just a few types of bead is classic, but you can make the sections sing and dance with bigger beads and lots of color. I suggest a color palette that emphasizes either cool or warm. Use contrast of color, shape, and size to create patterns within the sections. Try balancing busy sections with a short non-patterned length, as I did with the two sections of gold beads.

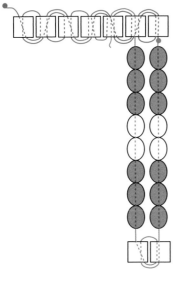

figure 1

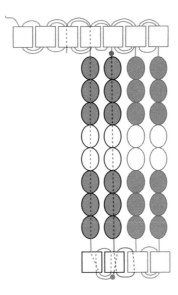

figure 2

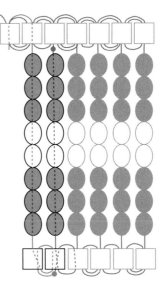

figure 3

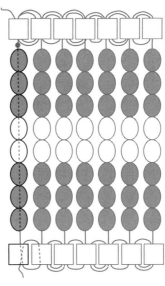

figure 4

NOTE I've started this bracelet at one end, but you can build out from a center ladder. This way, you can adjust the last sections equally to lengthen or shorten the bracelet.

1 **[Fig. 1, red thread]** Thread a needle on one end of a 3-yd. thread. Leaving a 10-in. tail, build a ladder of seven 3mm cube beads.

2 **[Fig. 1, blue thread]** Pick up the first pattern (three color A 8ºs, two color B 8ºs, and three color A 8ºs). Pick up two cubes, go through the first cube you picked up in the same direction, and pull the two cubes together to start a new ladder. Holding the two cubes in place, go again through the second cube. Pick up the first pattern, go back through the sixth cube added in the first ladder, turn, and go forward through the fifth cube added.

3 **[Fig. 2, red thread]** Pick up the first pattern plus a cube. Go back through the second cube in the second ladder, turn, and go forward through the cube just picked up.

4 **[Fig. 2, blue thread]** Pick up a cube, go forward through the third cube in the second ladder, turn, and go back through the new cube. Pick up the first pattern. Go back through the fourth cube in the first ladder, turn, and go forward through the third cube in the first ladder.

5 **[Fig. 3, red thread]** Repeat step 3, but go back through the fourth cube in the second ladder.

6 **[Fig. 3, blue thread]** Repeat step 4, but go forward through the fifth cube in the second ladder, and attach to the second and first cubes in the first ladder.

7 **[Fig. 4, red thread]** Pick up the first pattern plus a cube. Go back through the sixth cube of the second ladder and forward through the seventh cube. You are in position to start a new section.

8 Continue building sections until you reach the desired length. Change the patterns in each section to correspond to the sample shown, or invent your own. Sew a clasp on each end and end the threads.

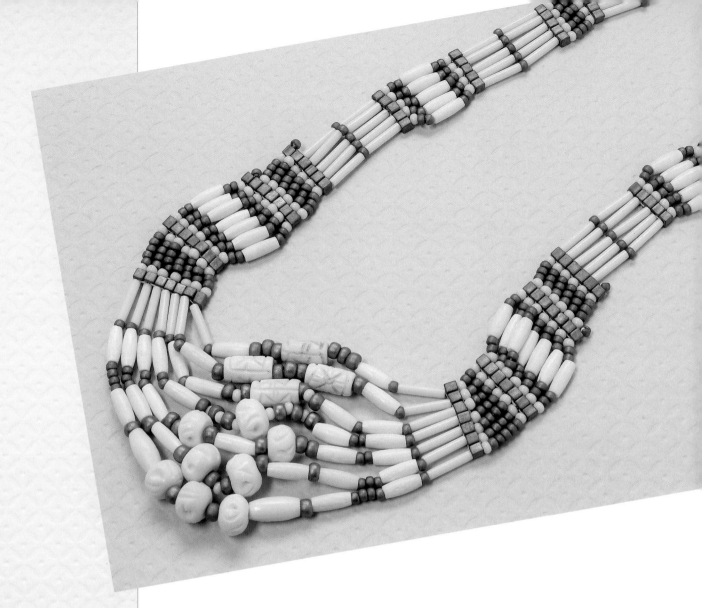

YOU'LL NEED:

- 110–140 3mm cube beads
- 70–80 12mm bugle beads
- 50–60 10mm oval beads
- 10–12 miscellaneous large accent beads
- 7g 8º seed beads in color A
- 3.5g 8º in color B
- 10–20 6º seed beads in color B (optional)
- clasp
- #10 needle
- 6 yd. thread

Tiered Necklace

The necklace follows the same technique as the bracelet: At the back, start with a narrow ladder of only three cubes. As you approach the center front, add rows to give the necklace more heft and presence. This piece is made in a casual African style using carved bone and neutral colors, but you can also make it glitter with shiny black cut glass and red accents for evening (see Gallery, p. 23).

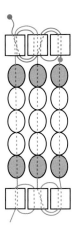

figure 1

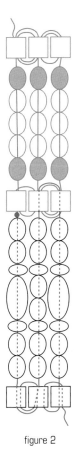

figure 2

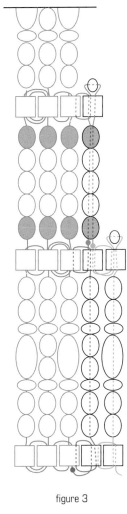

figure 3

1 [Fig. 1, red thread] Thread a needle on a 3-yd. thread. Leaving a 10-in. tail, build a ladder of three 3mm cube beads.

2 [Fig. 1, blue thread] Pick up the first pattern (in this example, a color B 8º, three color A 8ºs, and a color B 8º). Pick up two cubes, go again through the first cube you picked up in the same direction, and pull the two cubes together to start a new ladder. Holding the two cubes in place, go again through the second cube. Pick up the first pattern, go back through the second cube added in the first ladder, turn, and go forward through the first cube. Pick up the first pattern plus a cube. Go back through the second bead in the second ladder, and go forward through the cube you just picked up.

3 [Fig. 2] Repeat the technique in step 2 using a new pattern. Continue adding sections, increasing as described below, until you have the desired length of neck strap (about 7 in.).

INCREASING

4 [Fig. 3, red thread] To increase, work two sections past the point you want to increase. You will back up and increase in the last two sections. With your thread exiting the last cube in the newest ladder, pick up a cube, and attach it to the last cube. Pick up the pattern of the current section plus a cube. Attach the new cube to the nearest cube in the previous ladder.

5 [Fig. 3, blue thread] Pick up the pattern of the current section plus a cube. Attach the cube to the nearest cube in

the previous ladder. Pick up an 11º, turn, and go forward through the pattern you just picked up in this step.

6 [Fig. 3, orange thread] Go through the nearest cube in the next ladder. Attach a new cube to this cube, pick up an 11º, turn, and go forward through the next cube. Pick up the pattern of the current section plus a cube. Attach the new cube to the nearest cube in the next ladder.

FINISHING

7 When the first neck strap is the desired length, make a second neck strap in the same way to match. String beads between the two straps to join at the center, increasing as you go down each row to make a curve. Attach a clasp on each end, and end the threads.

NOTE   To join the two neck straps, I use a model or a display torso. Sew on the clasp and fasten it, or pin the two ends together at the back of the neck and drape it on the model as it would hang on your neck. Join the top row first and work down, increasing the number of beads a few per new row until your spacing is even and the drape is graceful.

YOU'LL NEED:

- 160–170 3mm cube beads in color A (dark)
- 85–90 3mm cubes in color B (light)
- 1g 11º seed beads in color A (dark)
- 1.5g 11ºs in color B (light)
- bar-and-loop clasp
- #10 needle
- 4¹/₂ yd. thread

Aztec Ladder Bracelet

This snaky bracelet reminds me of designs on an Aztec ruin, where the snake seems to ascend the steps of a great pyramid. The matching earrings are reminiscent of an ancient symbol. To make this piece, you will build a very long ladder. The trick is to keep the tension taut so the beads don't pull apart and show thread. You want your ladder to be snug but not rigid. Even tension is the key. I like to keep my thumb and forefinger clamped together on the last bead and the bead I'm adding to ensure that they don't pull apart while I'm sewing them in place.

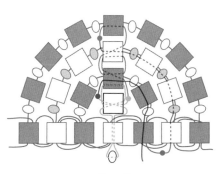

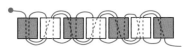

figure 1

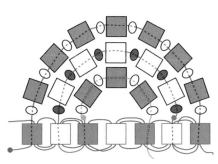

figure 2

figure 3

1 **[Fig. 1]** Thread a needle on 1½ yd. of thread and attach a stop bead, leaving a 10-in. tail. Build a ladder of 3mm cube beads that circles your wrist. The colors should start with A and alternate between A and B. A ladder of 51 beads makes a 7-in. bracelet after adding the clasp. To shorten or lengthen, drop or add beads in quantities of four. When you finish the length, leave the tails loose, or add a stop bead until you work the end.

2 **[Fig. 2, red thread]** Start a new thread 3 yd. long with a stop bead and a 10-in. tail. If you can't work with this length of thread, you can use 1½–2 yd. and add a new thread later. Come out the end cube in the base ladder going the opposite direction from the tail. Pick up an alternating pattern of a B 11º and an A cube until you have seven cubes and eight 11ºs. Go down through the seventh cube in the base ladder and up through the sixth cube.

3 **[Fig. 2, blue thread]** Pick up an alternating pattern of an A 11º and a B cube until you have five cubes and six 11ºs. Go down through the second cube in the base ladder and go up through the third cube.

4 **[Fig. 2, orange thread]** Pick up an alternating pattern of a B 11º and an A cube until you have three cubes and four 11ºs. Go down through the fifth cube of the base ladder. Check that all the rows are snug but not rigid.

5 **[Fig. 3, red thread]** Turn and go up through the center arc of bead cubes until you go through the center B cube of that arc.

6 **[Fig. 3, blue thread]** Attach the center A cube of the top arc to that B cube. Then attach the center A cube of the bottom arc to that B cube. Go through the center A cube of the bottom arc row again.

7 **[Fig. 3, orange thread]** Pick up a B cube, and go through the bottom arc A cube and the new B cube again. Go down through the B cube in the base ladder below the center of the arcs. Pick up a B 11º, turn, go back up through the B cube in the ladder, and go through the new B cube in the opposite direction.

8 **[Fig. 3, purple thread]** Turn and go back through the center A cube of the bottom arc, the rest of the arc, and all the way into the A cube in the base row. Flip the bracelet over, and you are in position to start the next arc.

9 Repeat this pattern across the base ladder. Use the end threads to make a short arc over the three base cubes at each end. Using the thread on the starting end of the bracelet, attach the loop of a bar-and-loop clasp. On the other end of the bracelet, pick up three B cubes and the bar. End the threads.

NOTE If you need to lengthen the bracelet, simply add another cube or two to the base ladder before attaching the clasp. To shorten the bracelet, stop short of the last arc and remove cubes from the base ladder.

MATCHING EARRINGS

To make a matching earring, build a ladder of seven cubes. Exit to one side of the center cube and build a ladder of three beads. Go back into the center cube, and repeat on the other side to make the fourth arm. String alternating cubes and 11ºs between the arms of the cross.

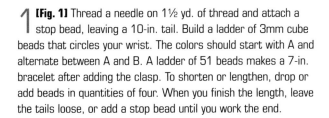

YOU'LL NEED:

- 38 3mm cube beads
- 16 6mm oval faceted beads or crystal bicones
- 34 $11^{\underline{0}}$ seed beads
- 2 3mm closed jump rings
- pair of ear wires
- #10 needle
- 2 yd. thread

Chandelier Earrings

These are substantial earrings and a little heavy, but they're so exciting!
When made with transparent or translucent beads, these chandeliers
seem to glow from the inside out. You could glamour them up even more
by adding a drop at the tip. Experiment with hanging various types of fringe
on the bottom half.

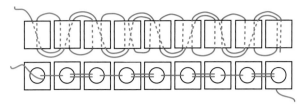

figure 1

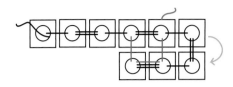

figure 2

MAKING THE BASE

1 **[Fig. 1]** Thread a needle on 1 yd. of thread. Build a ladder of nine 3mm cube beads.

2 **[Fig. 2]** Fold the last three cubes back against the middle three beads, and attach the last two beads to the fourth and fifth beads.

3 **[Fig. 3]** Fold the first three cubes back against the middle three cubes, and attach the first and second cubes to the fifth and sixth cubes. You should have a square base of nine cubes, all attached, and your thread should be coming out of a corner cube.

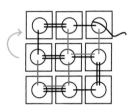

figure 3

MAKING THE TOP

4 **[Fig. 4]** Pick up a faceted bead, a cube, an 11º, a cube, and a closed jump ring. Go back through all the beads you just added and the corner cube you started from. Go up through the adjacent cube to the right in the base, pick up an 11º, and go back down through the same cube. Go up through the adjacent corner cube.

5 Pick up a faceted bead, a cube, and an 11º. Then sew through the last cube and closed jump ring added in step 4. Complete the rest of step 4, and repeat until you have built on all four corners of the base and added the final 11º. End the threads.

NOTE It's possible to get confused about which direction you are going around the outside of the base. Be sure to pick a direction and stick with it.

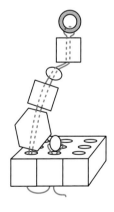

figure 4

MAKING THE BOTTOM

6 Repeat steps 4 and 5, but instead of turning through a closed jump ring, turn through a new 11º. End the thread.

NOTE If you are making this component to fit into a larger piece like a necklace, attach another jump ring to the bottom.

7 Attach an ear wire to the closed jump ring. Make another earring to match.

FRINGED CHANDELIERS

You can also make a fringed version of the chandelier earring. Just add drops or fringe to the bottom instead of a point. Here, I used a combination of long tubular beads ending with the same bicones as the top part of the chandelier.

Chandelier Necklace

You can use the components from the Chandelier Earrings as you would a large bead on a necklace or chain. If you attach closed jump rings to each end of the chandelier, you can attach it to other rings, to wire loops, to a chain, or to a wire with a crimp bead; you can also hang a pendant from the chandelier. This necklace uses all of these techniques for truly beautiful results!

1 Make three chandeliers following steps 1–7 in Chandelier Earrings, p. 18, all with bases of 3mm cube beads. On two of them, make the points with a pattern of a 6mm pearl, a 3mm crystal bicone, a cube, and a closed jump ring at both ends. Make the third central chandelier with a pattern of a pear-shaped faceted bead, a 2mm bicone, a cube, and closed jump rings. For all three, fill the center cube hole on each side of the base with matching 11ºs. End the thread.

2 Using eyepins, string two segments of two pearls separated by a metallic spacer, making a plain loop on the remaining end of each eyepin.

3 Attach a pendant to one end of the central chandelier. Attach both eyepin segments to the other end of the central chandelier and to the two remaining chandeliers.

4 Attach flexible beading wire to the free end of one of the two chandeliers using a crimp bead. String it with matching beads to the desired length and attach to the other chandelier using a crimp bead. Or you can attach a chain to the two chandeliers instead of the strung wire.

NOTE You can substitute faceted ovals, pear shapes, or ovals of glass or stone for the faceted round beads or bicones in the chandeliers. Just be sure your choice of bead is not too large to fit on top of the nine-bead base.

BLACK AND RED TIERED NECKLACE

For those who love the sparkle of crystal, here is a perfect combination of faceted glass and 4mm square crystal beads. The cubes make a solid base for the necklace to build on, and the faceted black crystals do their magic to make this a special evening look. Under a cluster of ovals, a crystal chandelier pendant takes center stage.

GREEN BRACELET

Build a wide, free-form piece using your favorite colors. I included a multicolored gemstone strand to give the bracelet body and variations in shades.

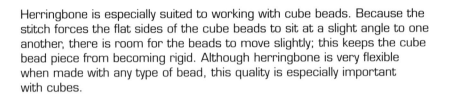

Herringbone Stitch

Herringbone is especially suited to working with cube beads. Because the stitch forces the flat sides of the cube beads to sit at a slight angle to one another, there is room for the beads to move slightly; this keeps the cube bead piece from becoming rigid. Although herringbone is very flexible when made with any type of bead, this quality is especially important with cubes.

I also find herringbone easier to work with using cubes. Round seed beads are quite slippery, so cube beads offer a great way for beginners to tackle the stitch.

The flat surfaces of the cube beads seem to enhance the herringbone texture. Each side of the bead is like a facet that picks up the movement of the beads. There are ways to enhance this by using contrasting combinations, such as matte and glossy.

Once you've learned the basics of herringbone, the sky's the limit! You may substitute a different sort of bead for one of the cubes, as shown in Seed Stitch Bracelet (p. 25). Seed stitch is a crochet term for a stitch that has a little picot of thread that stands out to give a seeded look. By replacing every other cube with a round seed bead, you can get a similar effect. This bracelet can be made with any size of cube. I've shown a number of examples to get you started.

But we're not done with herringbone yet, because there is more you can do—try adding beads between the pairs in a row of herringbone, as I've done in the Fancy Herringbone Cuff (p. 29). You can also use different sizes of cubes to create a curve: Stitch a smaller cube along one side of a herringbone band, and the smaller side will contract and draw the band into an arc. Start at the bottom and work up each side with an arc to the upper middle, then join them together into a symmetrical circle.

For a paisley shape, curve the arc back onto itself. These shapes can be joined in a number of ways to make a bracelet or necklace.

I've played with the characteristics of herringbone in all the sizes of cube beads. Whether it's a chunky piece with 4mm cubes or a refined piece with 1.5mm cubes, herringbone always creates a piece of jewelry that is full of interest and movement.

Seed Stitch Bracelet

This big-bead bracelet provides an easy way for a beginner to learn herringbone stitch. The silver and purple bracelet on the left uses 4mm cubes with 6⁰ seed beads, as in the instructions. If you are more advanced, choose any size of cube with a matching seed bead size: With 3mm cubes, use 8⁰ seed beads; with 2mm cubes, use either 8⁰ or 11⁰; and with 1.5 or 1.8mm cubes, use 11⁰ seed beads. The beads alternate both horizontally and vertically, so the stitch accommodates two sizes.

You can also make this pattern into a fashionable cuff. Simply increase the beginning row of ladder stitched cube beads to any even number—10 is a good width for a cuff using 3mm cubes—and work herringbone the same all the way across. If you like a more delicate look, choose smaller beads for a narrower size.

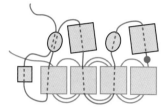

figure 1

figure 2

figure 3

 Experiment with the type of bead you alternate with the cubes; try combining glossy dark blue 3mm cubes and matte gold 8º hex beads.

1 **[Fig. 1]** Thread the needle on one end of a 2½ yd. thread and build a ladder of four 4mm cubes. I like to go ahead and attach the loop part of the bar-and-loop clasp to the center of the ladder. Leave the short tail loose to end later.

2 **[Fig. 2]** With the working thread, pick up a 4mm and a 6º seed bead; go down through the adjacent 4mm in the ladder and up through the 4mm next to that. Pick up a 4mm and a 6º, and go down through the last bead in the ladder. Pick up a 2mm cube bead and go up through the 6º you last exited.

3 **[Fig. 3]** Turn the work so the surface that was facing you as you worked the row in step 2 is now facing away from you. The working thread should still be at the top of the work and the ladder at the bottom. Repeat step 2. Continue to turn and repeat until you reach the desired length. Make the last row all 4mms and sew back through it as though it were a ladder, pulling all the 4mms tight against each other. Sew on the other end of the clasp, and end the threads.

DESIGN ELEMENT: TEXTURE

Texture in general can be quite subtle, giving a satin or matte finish, or texture can be bold, such as the addition of nubs on fabric, or clusters of fiber as in a berber carpet. In beadwork as well, texture creates surface interest.

In this bracelet, I created texture by several means. The herringbone itself makes a texture in the way the beads angle back and forth. I added a second textural quality by changing the beads to two different shapes—cube and round. And finally, I created even more texture by choosing alternating qualities on the surfaces of the beads, such as matte, glossy, iridescent, and metallic, that contrast to give even more surface interest.

A good textural effect is a lovely thing! I like to just let it speak for itself without much distraction.

Patterned Herringbone Bracelets

Herringbone isn't often used with a pattern, but it works quite well; you can make a complex-looking bracelet design with ease. For the main piece, I combined texture with an easy pattern. The center section alternates a shiny silver metallic cube with a clear matte silver-lined cube of the same size. The accent consists of a matte black cube strip along each edge. It's simple, but so elegant. The yellow bracelet on p. 28 uses nothing but color change to make a pattern. The challenge is to get the pattern exactly right. Play around with color combinations as well as bead size.

**FOR THE SILVER &
BLACK BRACELET,
YOU'LL NEED:**

- 2g 1.5mm cube beads in color A (black)
- 5g 1.5mm cubes in color B (silver metallic)
- 4g 1.5mm cubes in color C (silver-lined matte)
- 1g 15º seed beads in color B
- clasp
- #10 needle
- 8 yd. thread

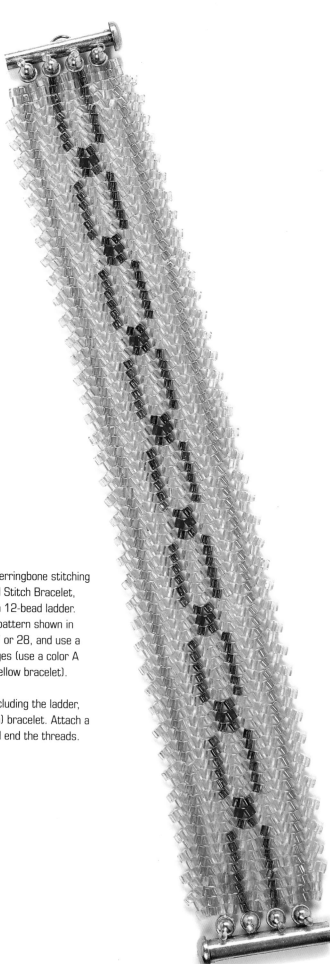

FOR THE YELLOW BRACELET, YOU'LL NEED:

- 7g 1.5mm cube beads in color A (yellow)
- 2g 1.5mm cubes in color B (light gray)
- 2g 1.5mm cubes in color C (dark gray)
- 16 1.5mm cubes in color D (red)
- clasp
- #10 needle
- 8 yd. thread

1 Follow the same herringbone stitching pattern as in Seed Stitch Bracelet, p. 25, but start with a 12-bead ladder. Follow the cube bead pattern shown in the bracelets on p. 27 or 28, and use a 15º to turn on the edges (use a color A 1.5mm cube for the yellow bracelet).

2 Work 80 rows, including the ladder, for an 8-in. (20cm) bracelet. Attach a clasp to each end, and end the threads.

Fancy Herringbone Cuff

When you work herringbone, you can insert different kinds of beads between the pairs. In this bold cuff, I inserted larger beads and smaller beads, alternating between the pairs to create exciting texture and pattern. The larger beads also add a new shape of bead and a new color combination to the mix. Alternating colors down the center of the bracelet adds one more layer of interest.

I'm also showing you a way to make your own clasp. Wide clasps are somewhat hard to find. The best choice I've found is the 5- or 6-ring slide lock clasp, but I've included an easy wireworked clasp design in this project. In principle, it is a safety pin; it attaches two tubes of peyote stitch that you sew to the ends of the bracelet.

YOU'LL NEED:

- 8g 3mm cube beads in color A (dark brown)
- 12g 3mm cubes in color B (gold)
- 2.5g 11º seed beads
- 42–50 4mm glass beads
- #10 needle
- 6 yd. thread

1 [Fig. 1, red thread] Thread a needle on one end of a 3-yd. length of thread. Build a ladder of 3mm cube beads in the following pattern: ABAABAABAABA.

2 [Fig. 1, blue thread] Pick up an A and a B. Go down through the second cube of the ladder, up through the third cube, down through the fourth cube, and up through the fifth cube. Pick up a B and an A. Go down through the sixth cube and up through the seventh cube. Pick up two Bs, and go down, up, down, and up as before. Pick up a B and an A, and go down through the last cube in the ladder. Pick up two 11°s and go up through the last cube added.

3 [Fig. 2, red thread] Pick up an A and a B, and go down through the B below. Pick up three 11°s and go up through the next B over. Pick up a B and an A, and go down the B below, and up through the adjacent A. Pick up two Bs and go down through the B below. Pick up three 11°s and go up through the next B in the row. Pick up a B and an A, and go down through the last A. Pick up two 11°s and go up through the last cube added.

4 [Fig. 2, blue thread] Pick up an A and a B, and go down through the B below. Pick up a 4mm bead, go up through the next B over, pick up a B and an A, go down through the next B over, and go up through the adjacent A. Pick up two Bs and go down through the B below. Pick up a 4mm and go up through the next B. Pick up a B and an A, and go down through the last A. Pick up two 11°s and go up through the last cube you added.

5 Repeat steps 3 and 4.

6 Stop after you have attached a row with 4mms. For the last row, go through the same cubes added in the previous row without adding any new cubes (still adding the two sets of three 11°s). Make a final row of all cubes to mirror the ladder on the starting end, and sew back through the ladder of cubes.

YOU'LL NEED:

- 3g 11° seed beads
- #10 needle
- 1 yd. thread
- $3^{1}/_{2}$ in. hard wire
- heavy wire cutters
- roundnose pliers
- file (optional)

ADDING A WIRE CLASP

You will need a hard, springy wire—not pure silver or sterling wire, as those metals are too soft. Bronze 18-gauge or well-tumbled Argentium sterling silver 16-gauge wire will work. Or, you can cut down a large safety pin or even a paper clip, but please cut all of these wires with a pair of industrial wire cutters, or you will ruin your nice fine-wire cutters.

1 Bend the wire to the pin shape as shown in the photo. File the ends round to take off any burs, if needed.

2 Attach two 11°s onto each of the eight center cubes at one end of the bracelet. Use these beads as the base for a strip of two-drop peyote. Make the strip seven or eight rows long and zip it to the first row to make a tube. Repeat this step at the other end of the bracelet, but **insert the wire pin before zipping it up**.

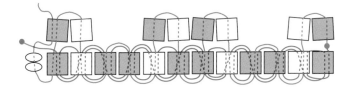

figure 1

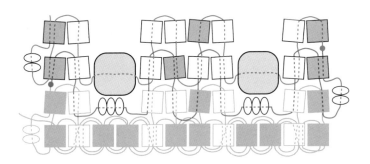

figure 2

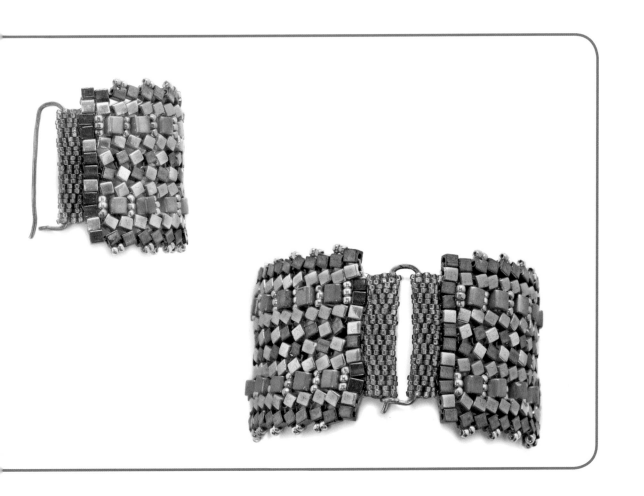

YOU'LL NEED:

- 22 3mm cube beads in color A (olive green metallic matte)
- 20 3mm cubes in color B (bronze-lined peridot)
- 24 2mm cubes in color A
- 26 2mm cubes in color B
- 58 11º seed beads (cabernet galvanized matte)
- 4 11º seed beads (green)
- 2 3mm closed jump rings
- pair of ear wires
- 2 #10 needles
- 2 yd. thread

Wreath Earrings

A wreath is one of the first things one might do with a ring of beads. I searched for the right color combination and found that not one but two colors made it work. The fresh, pungent greenery and red berries of the holidays inspired the color choices. If you want these earrings for year-round wear, a bold black-and-white version really pops. Or choose your favorite color and pair it with a metallic for contrast.

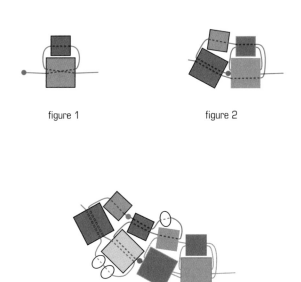

figure 1

figure 2

figure 3

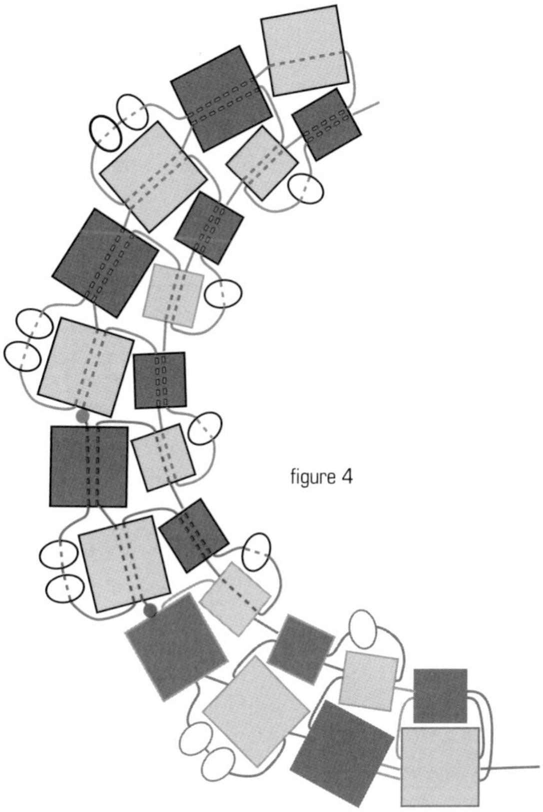

figure 4

NOTE In these instructions, cube beads are called 3A or B (3mm in color A and B) and 2A or B (2mm in color A and B).

1 **[Fig. 1]** Thread needles on both ends of a yard of thread. Pick up a 3B and a 2A. Go again in the same direction through the 3B. Center the pair of beads on the thread.

2 **[Fig. 2]** With the thread going to the left, pick up a 3A and a 2B. Go back through the first 2A, forward through the first 3B, and on through the new 3A. Take out any slack.

3 **[Fig. 3, red thread]** Pick up a 3B and a 2A, and go back through the previous 2B. Pick up an 11º, turn, and go forward through the 2A you just picked up.

4 **[Fig. 3, blue thread]** Pick up a 2B and a 3A; go back through the previous 3B. Pick up two 11ºs and go forward through the 3A you just picked up.

NOTE At every step, check that the work is tight and the cubes are aligned as in the illustration. Turn the work if it helps, but don't let the turning loosen the work.

5 **[Fig. 4, red thread]** Pick up a 3B and a 2A; go back through the previous 2B. Align the two beads, pick up an 11º, and go forward through the 2A you just picked up. Pick up a 2B and a 3A. Go back through the previous 3B, pick up two 11ºs, and go forward through the new 3A.

6 **[Fig. 4, blue thread]** Repeat the pattern from step 5 two more times, and then pick up a 3B and a 2A; go back through the previous 2B. Align the two beads, pick up an 11º, and go forward through the 2A you just picked up. You now have 10 3mm cubes around the outside edge (not including the starting 3B).

7 Thread a needle on the other end of the thread and repeat from step 2 to create an arc for the other side of the wreath.

8 **[Fig. 5]** With either thread, pick up a 2B; go through the 2A of the opposite side and continue all the way around the opposite side of the ring, going through all the 2mm cubes, including the starting 2A. With the other thread, go through the new 2A and on through all the 2mm cubes on the other side until you meet the first thread at the bottom of the wreath. Pull both threads taut to equalize the tension and tie a surgeon's knot.

NOTE These beads have large holes, and this causes them to wobble a bit on their threads. You want your wreath to hold its shape, so the more times you go through the beads, the stiffer the wreath will become.

9 **[Fig. 6, red thread]** With one thread, go back through the bottom center 2A, pulling the knot into the bead to hide it. Take each of the threads outward through the 2Bs, turn, and go inward through the 3As. With one thread, pick up three 11ºs, and cross the other needle through them. With both needles, go outward through the 3As to both sides.

10 **[Fig. 6, blue thread]** Go up through all the 3mm cubes on that side. Mirror the same path with the other thread. Now your threads will be coming out the two top 3mms.

11 **[Fig. 6, orange thread]** With one thread, pick up a 2B and a 2A. Attach the 2A to the top center 2B below it; that is, go through it and come out where you started. With the other thread, pick up a 2B, and go through the 2A you just added. You are ready to attach the jump ring.

NOTE The way I attach the jump ring keeps it held taut in the plane of the earring, so your wreath will always be facing front. If it wants to lie down flat against the beads, don't worry; just don't pull the attaching threads very tight, and the weight of the earring will straighten it up once it's attached to the ear wire.

12 **[Fig. 6, orange thread]** To attach the jump ring, pick up a green 11º and the ring with either thread and go back through the 11º and the center 2A. Repeat with the other thread. You can repeat both passes again in order to have four threads attaching to the jump ring.

13 Finally, with both threads, go through all the 2mm cubes on each side until they meet at the middle of the bottom. End each thread.

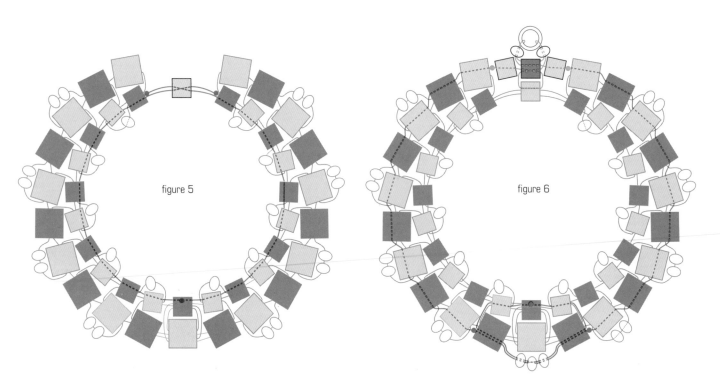

figure 5

figure 6

Oval Earrings

Make a bold statement with this pair of earrings. Because they are large and open, they may need some stiffening. You'll find this technique included in the instructions. Use one color of bead, like the beautiful bronze-lined aqua, or you can use the 11⁰ turnaround beads as an accent color. I've done these in matte black with gold 11⁰ beads, and in iridescent navy blue with silver 11⁰ beads.

MAKE THE EARRINGS

Follow the Wreath Earrings instructions, p. 32, but make the following changes: Add about a foot more thread to start each earring and use just one color of 3mm and 2mm cubes. Work the pattern until you have 14 3mm cubes on each side. This will make the herringbone ring long enough to stretch into an oval. Instead of closing the ring with three 2mm cubes at the top, add only one 3mm, crossing through one cube to add the two 11°s and jump ring. End the thread.

STIFFENING

Because this ring is longer and looser, it may need some help staying in shape. You can make another pass through all the beads, being careful not to pull the outer rows of 3mms tighter than the inner rows of 2mms, or the piece will warp. If this does not work sufficiently, you can try to stiffen it with other products.

Here's one way of doing that: Find a piece of thin, clear plastic or any kind of paper product that blends with your colors. Cut an oval ring just smaller than the earring, rough up one side with fine sandpaper and glue that side to the back of the earring, holding the oval shape until it sets.

An alternative is to carefully dab glue at the joints on the back side, but be sure that you have a clear glue that it is not so thin that it seeps through to the other side.

Some beaders are familiar with this method. Lay the earring, back down, into a thin layer of acrylic floor finish (Pledge brand works well). Leave it in the wax long enough that it begins to set. Take it out and lay it on a piece of waxed paper or other nonstick surface and let it dry completely.

Flame of India Earrings

Adding a little "fire" to the Oval Earrings gives them an exotic look. These remind me of something a dancer in an ancient temple might wear as she performs her graceful, mysterious moves. The beads used are the smaller 1.5mm and 2mm cubes, giving it a more refined look, though not less dramatic. I've also changed the way the earring attaches to the ear wire.

YOU'LL NEED:

- 58 2mm cube beads (gold)
- 60 1.5mm cubes (gold)
- 80 11^0 seed beads (gold)
- 36 11^0 seed beads (ruby silver lined)
- 26 15^0 seed beads (gold metallic)
- 8 2mm glass faceted ovals
- 8 4mm glass faceted ovals
- 2 6mm glass faceted ovals
- 2 3mm closed jump rings
- pair of ear wires
- 2 #10 needles
- $2^2/_3$ yd. thread

1 **[Fig. 1]** This earring starts the same as the Wreath Earrings, p. 32, but you will be using 2mm cube beads on the outside and 1.5mm cubes on the inside, and all the cubes are the same color. You'll also add about a foot more thread to start each earring. Increase the sides to a count of 14 2mms. When you finish both sides through step 6 of Wreath Earrings, cross both threads through a 1.5mm cube and take both threads down through all the 1.5mms on each side to the bottom and tie them in a dry knot next to the bottom center 1.5mm. Pull the knot into the center cube with the appropriate thread.

2 **[Fig. 2, blue thread]** With either thread, continue through the next 1.5mm; turn and go back through the adjacent two 2mms. Pick up three 11º seed beads, a 6mm faceted oval, and a 15º seed bead; turn and go back up through the faceted oval. Pick up two 11ºs and go through the corresponding two 2mms on the other side of the ring. Turn, go down through two 11ºs, and pick up an 11º, a 4mm faceted oval, and a 15º. Go back up through the faceted oval and three 11ºs. Go up through two 2mms and two 11ºs.

3 **[Fig. 2, green thread]** Work your way up the entire side, going up through two 2mms, down through the two 11ºs, and picking up some "fire" in the form of an accent dangle. The order of the accent dangles after the center 6mm dangle is: an 11º, a 4mm, and a 15º; a 4mm and a 15º; an 11º, a 2mm, and a 15º; a 2mm and a 15º; and a red 11º and a 15º for the last two dangles. Repeat this pattern with the other thread up the other side.

4 **[Fig. 2, purple thread]** Repeat steps 2–4, taking the other thread through the existing 11º, 6mm, and 15º you added with the last beads.

5 When your threads meet at the top, cross them through a single 11º and take both through the opposite 2mms. With either thread, pick up three 11ºs and a jump ring. Come back through the three 11ºs and back through the 2mm you exited.

Repeat with the other thread, going through the existing jump ring. Run each thread through the center 11º again and down through all the 2mms on each side to the bottom center. End the threads.

6 Make a second earring to match. Attach each earring to an ear wire.

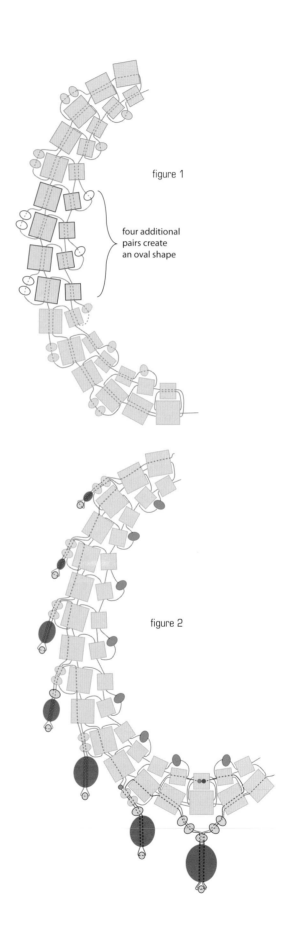

figure 1

four additional pairs create an oval shape

figure 2

Linked Circles
Bracelet

This bracelet is made using the same technique as the Wreath Earrings,
p. 32, except you stop short of closing the circle and start a new circle in
a different color. Choose contrasting bead colors to really see the design.
The blue-and-gold bracelet is made using 3mm and 2mm cubes, but you
can also make a version using 2mm and 1.5mm as shown in the silver-
and-black example. Just substitute the smaller cubes and use 15⁰s instead
of 11⁰s for the turnaround beads.

YOU'LL NEED:

- 60–65 3mm cube
  beads in color A
- 65–70 3mm cubes in
  color B
- 85–90 2mm cubes in
  color A
- 85–90 2mm cubes in
  color B
- 1g 11⁰ seed beads in
  color A
- 1g 11⁰ seed beads in
  color B
- bar-and-loop clasp
- 3¹⁄₂ yd. thread
- 2 #10 needles

NOTE In these instructions, cube beads are called 3A or B (3mm in color A and B) and 2A or B (2mm in color A and B), and seed beads are called 11º A or B. For steps 1–3, refer to the illustrations for the Wreath Earrings, p. 32.

1 Thread a needle on each end of 3½ yd. of thread. With either needle, pick up a 3A and a 2A. Go again through the 3A, pull the 2A side-by-side against the 3mm, and center the joined beads on the thread. (You can sew on the loop side of the clasp before you continue or do so later, as shown in the **figure**).

2 With either thread, * pick up a 3A and a 2A. Go back through the center 2A, turn, and go through the center 3A and the 3A you just added.

3 Pick up a 3A and a 2A. Go back through the last 2A, pick up an 11ºA, turn, and go forward through the 2A you just picked up. Pick up a 2A and a 3A. Go back through the last 3A, pick up two 11ºAs, turn, and go forward through the 3A you just added.

NOTE Keeping the tension taut will serve you well here. It is easy to lose it on this short curved section, so I recommend that you keep the thread wound around your third finger while you work, as in crochet, and reattach it as soon as you've finished an action.

4 Repeat step 3 until you have just added the third set of two 11ºs and gone forward through the 3A. At this point, pick up two 2As and go back through the 2A in the previous row. Pick up an 11ºA and go forward through the 2A on the same side.

5 Repeat step 2 from * through the end of step 4 with the other thread. At this point you will be ready to start the second circle in color B.

6 **[Fig., red and blue threads]** With either thread, pick up a 2A, a 3B, and a 2B, go through the 3B again, and pull the 2B side-by-side with the 3B. Take up all the slack and pull these two beads firmly together. Repeat the action with the other thread using the same beads. Repeat step 2 with both threads and B color beads, adding a 3B and 2B to each side.

7 **[Fig., green thread]** Pick up a 3B and a 2B, go back through the previous 2B, pick up an 11ºB, turn, and go forward through the 2B you just added. Pick up a 2B and a 3B, and go back through the previous 3B. Go through the 2A of the last pair added in the previous A circle, taking the needle from the inward side to the outward side of the bead, pick up two 11ºBs, and continue forward through the 3B you just added. Continue the stitch as in steps 3 and 4. Repeat on the other side as in step 5. Add a new circle by working steps 6 and 7 with A beads.

CONTRAST

There are a number of ways to create contrast in your beadwork. The most obvious is color contrast—that is, the colors are so different that they stand out from each other. For example, you may choose a warm against a cool color, such as red against green, or orange against purple.

But you may notice that sometimes the two colors don't contrast as much as they could. This is probably because they are of the same value. Value refers to the amount of light or dark in a color. You can think of value in terms of black and white, as if you are mixing colors. Pink, for example is a lighter value of red, as if you mixed it with white. Wine is a darker version of red, as if you mixed it with black. This can affect the contrast greatly. So if you choose two pastel colors, you may not get the contrast you're looking for, even though those colors are opposite on the color wheel. In the blue-and-gold example, there is just enough contrast for the design to work.

Another factor in the blue-and-gold bracelet is that both beads have glossy surfaces. In the black-and-silver bracelet, the surface quality is used as contrast, too: light against dark, black against silver, and matte against shiny. This is probably the maximum amount of contrast you can attain with beads.

Glossy finishes cut the color and value of any bead choice. That's why I don't use a lot of them. When the light hits a glossy finish, you often see more of the white light bouncing back at your eyes than you do of the color embedded under the gloss.

8 Continue to add circles, changing colors in every new circle. When you get to the last round, continue the sides until you have added the fourth set of two 11ºs and gone through the 3mm you just added. With either thread, pick up a 3mm and a 2mm, and go through the 3mm again. Lock the two beads together side-by-side. Take the other thread through the same beads in the same pattern but from the other side, creating two new center beads for the end. Take out any slack.

9 Attach the bar side of the clasp by sewing in and out of the center 3mm from each side and into the clasp. (Don't forget to add a few beads to extend the bar so it will clasp.)

10 When you have finished sewing on the clasp, take both threads into the center 2mm from their respective sides, crossing them in the 2mm, and continue to sew through all the 2mm cubes on each side until your threads meet on the other side of the last circle. End the thread.

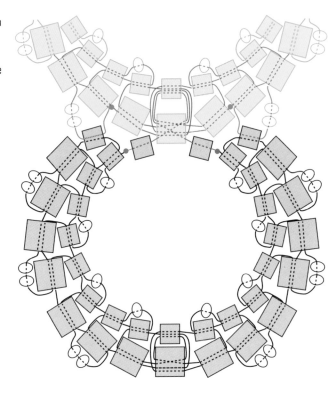

figure

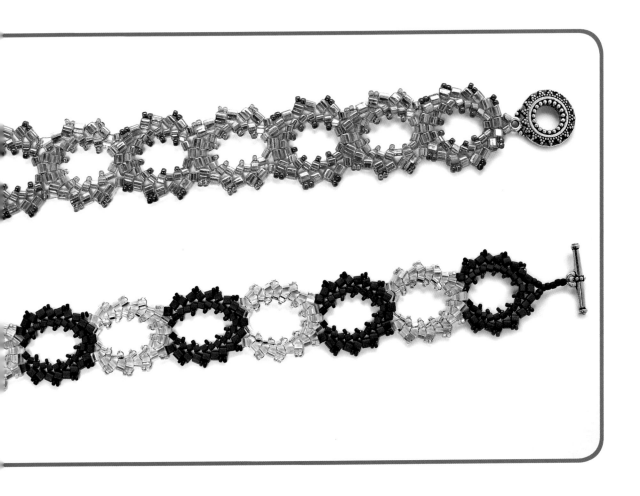

Paisley Earrings

I thought I had finished with curved herringbone earrings, but this one surprised me. I can see this shape used as a fabric decoration along with other beadwork or incorporated into some bead embroidery. I hope you have fun with this!

1 Follow the instructions for Wreath Earrings, p. 32, with these exceptions: Substitute 1.5mm cubes for the 2mms and 2mm cubes for the 3mms, and use the same color for both sizes. Pick up an 11º between the beads of each pair, including the two starting beads. Turn around using only one 11º instead of pairs along the outside. Follow these new instructions as you go:

2 **[Fig., black thread]** Work one side until you have 18 2mm cubes on the outside (not including the starting 2mm); then work one more stitch with a 1.5mm cube, an 11º, and a 1.5mm cube. After you pick up the turnaround bead, go down to the tip, through the last center 11º, and up through all the 1.5mms to the top, stopping just before you go through the center starting 1.5mm.

3 **[Fig., black thread]** With the other thread, work the second side the same as the wreath until you have seven 2mms along the outside; then work a stitch with a 1.5mm, an 11º, and a 1.5mm.

4 **[Fig., red thread]** Reverse the position of the cubes, putting the 2mm on the inside and the 1.5mm on the outside. Work

YOU'LL NEED:
- 60 2mm cube beads
- 68 1.5mm cubes
- 1.5g 11º seed beads
- 2 3mm closed jump rings
- pair of ear wires
- 3 yd. thread
- 2 #10 needles

until you have four 2mms along the inside edge, but don't pick up the last turnaround bead.

JOINING THE TWO SIDES

5 **[Fig., blue thread]** Instead of picking up the turnaround bead, go down through the seventh 11º on the first side, down through the cube you just came out of, down through the next 11º (the eighth on the first side), down through the next 2mm on the other side below the one you started from, and then down through the next 11º (the ninth).

6 **[Fig., orange thread]** Turn and go up through two 2mms on this side, turn, and go down through an 11º and two 1.5mms on the first side. Continue through the next 11º, turn, and go through all the 2mm cubes along the top of the first side, exiting next to the other thread.

7 To attach an ear wire, tie a knot, cross both threads through the top center 2mm, and attach a closed jump ring from either side of the center 2mm, as in step 12 of the Wreath Earrings. End the thread.

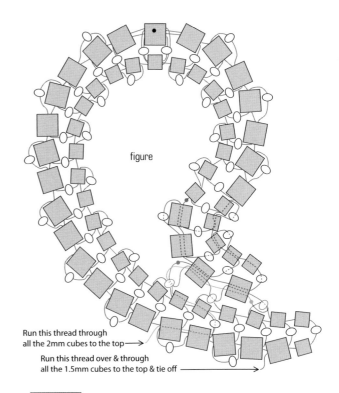

figure

Run this thread through all the 2mm cubes to the top→

Run this thread over & through all the 1.5mm cubes to the top & tie off —→

NOTE If your piece is loose, you can run more circuits through the 1.5mms and 2mms to tighten it, but don't pull the outside row of 2mm cubes tighter than the inside row of 1.5mm cubes.

ALTERNATIVE BRACELET OR NECKLACE

Join a series of paisley shapes together to make a graceful bracelet or necklace. Just make the individual paisley pieces that you need, laying them out in the placement you want. Run another thread through the outside (2mm) cubes and connect the paisley pieces at selected points where the turnaround beads project. As you join the pieces, add crystals or other beads between the turnaround beads for additional accents.

I attached mine by making an S-shaped connection, taking the thread out of the turnaround bead on one paisley, through the connecting bead or beads, into a turnaround bead on the other paisley, back through the connecting bead(s) and into the original turnaround bead from the opposite direction. Then I moved to the next connection.

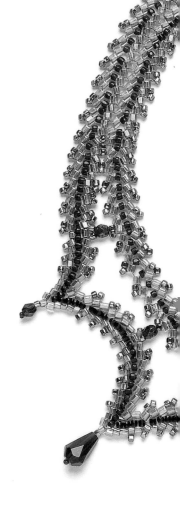

BLUE/GREEN
BAROQUE NECKLACE

Here, I've worked the curved herringbone into an open lacy look. I started with six-bead-wide rows of herringbone at the back and worked forward, splitting the upper section off and crossing it at the center. I made the blue center section, and then I went back and picked up the lower herringbone strand and developed the green outer section, working around the blue center section and attaching dangles and crystals as I went along. The crystals secure and strengthen the curves against the overall weight of the piece. The curved sections work the arcs back and forth to result in a graceful flourish.

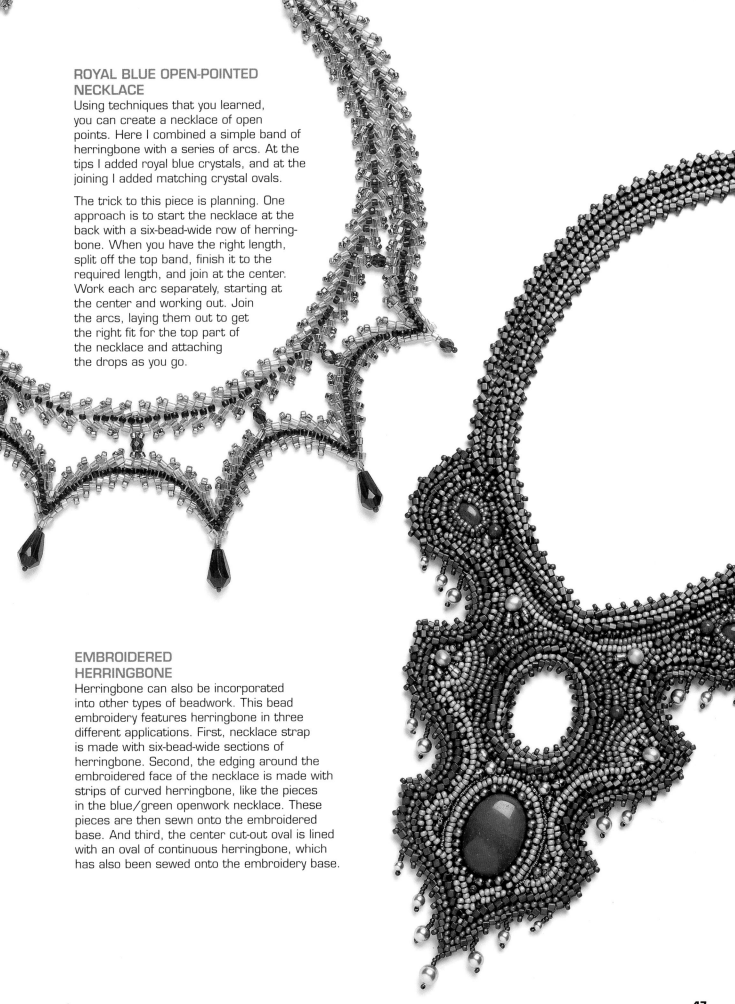

ROYAL BLUE OPEN-POINTED NECKLACE

Using techniques that you learned, you can create a necklace of open points. Here I combined a simple band of herringbone with a series of arcs. At the tips I added royal blue crystals, and at the joining I added matching crystal ovals.

The trick to this piece is planning. One approach is to start the necklace at the back with a six-bead-wide row of herringbone. When you have the right length, split off the top band, finish it to the required length, and join at the center. Work each arc separately, starting at the center and working out. Join the arcs, laying them out to get the right fit for the top part of the necklace and attaching the drops as you go.

EMBROIDERED HERRINGBONE

Herringbone can also be incorporated into other types of beadwork. This bead embroidery features herringbone in three different applications. First, necklace strap is made with six-bead-wide sections of herringbone. Second, the edging around the embroidered face of the necklace is made with strips of curved herringbone, like the pieces in the blue/green openwork necklace. These pieces are then sewn onto the embroidered base. And third, the center cut-out oval is lined with an oval of continuous herringbone, which has also been sewed onto the embroidery base.

Step Stitch

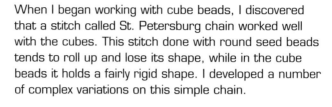

When I began working with cube beads, I discovered that a stitch called St. Petersburg chain worked well with the cubes. This stitch done with round seed beads tends to roll up and lose its shape, while in the cube beads it holds a fairly rigid shape. I developed a number of complex variations on this simple chain.

St. Petersburg chain is a simple stitch that can be found in the famous Russian "white book"—actually entitled The Art of Beadweaving by M. Ya. Anufrieva. The mirrored chain is where I began working with the stitch. I developed a variation using small cube beads that let me put a double-size cube down the center. This turned into earrings, bracelets, and necklaces. Then I developed a method of opening up the chain by alternating a center bead or beads with an open space. I also worked with color to create pattern and stripes.

From there, I developed a number of pieces that use short segments of the basic mirror but open it up to insert other stitches, making a tree, a heart, and a petal. Then further, I developed a radiating design in which the short segments of mirrored chain emerge off a ring of beads to form shapes like stars and flowers.

At this point, the title "St. Petersburg Chain" seemed inadequate. This technique was no longer just a chain, but more of a stitch. The original name of the stitch in Russian is "stepped stitch." You can look at the stitch and see how the name fits, so I've called my variations "step stitch" designs.

I have been expanding on the radiating patterns, working with double layers of petals and different numbers of points radiating from the center ring or from a square. I've worked with step stitch points radiating out along the edge of a peyote collar.

In step stitch, you always have two beads that double back and lock against two previous beads to form a small box of four beads. I call the beads that double back the "return" beads. These boxes are held together by picking up a couple of "turnaround" beads, as I call them, usually smaller than the primary bead size. These turnaround beads act somewhat like rivets to lock the box together.

There is more than one version of the simple chain. This depends on how many beads you pick up each time and where you double back. In the Russian version, you pick up four beads, turn back, and go through the previous two beads you picked up. Then you pick up a turnaround bead, go down through the three beads behind it, pick up another turnaround bead, and go out through the two return beads, then start over.

In my step chain, you start by picking up four beads, but thereafter the pattern develops differently. You pick up three beads (not four), and go again through the nearest bead in the previous box plus the third bead back from the needle. This joins the little four-bead boxes by overlapping one bead. Then you pick up a turnaround bead, go down through two beads (not three), pick up another turnaround bead, and exit through the two return beads.

The overall effect is that my chain is a bit narrower and tighter. This was an effect that I liked, and it led me to work with the chain in ways that metal chains are often used. However, both methods create a beautiful rope or lariat.

Mirrored chain is what I call the combination of two simple chains in a symmetrical relationship joined by one or more beads down the middle. Some of the many possibilities for mirrored step chain are shown in the bracelets in this section.

I introduced the radiating step stitch in my first book to make a star, snowflakes, and a medallion. It begins with a ring of 11° beads, and points of step stitch radiate out from that center. In this book I use it for a new five-pointed star, beautiful white poinsettias, a blue starflower, and an array of other points, petals and leaves. You can use a point or leaf of step stitch in all sorts of places, as seen in the three pairs of crystal earrings.

The expanded step stitch variation came about when I started incorporating Tila beads into my stitching. This variation simply extends the number of little boxes to make a wider version of the chain.

Chains Necklace

FOR A 70-IN. NECKLACE, YOU'LL NEED:

- 15g 1.5 or 1.8mm cube beads
- 5g 15º seed beads
- 2 1-in metal rings
- 10 3mm jump rings
- clasp
- #10 needle
- thread
- two pairs of chainnose pliers

Any design that uses a metal chain can be replicated with a step stitch chain. This version is similar to a current popular style. I've used large rings to link several chains together, but you could also use some of the beautiful multiple-ring findings now available. This is a great way to become familiar with this stitch. Once you've made all these chains, step stitch will be second nature.

MAKING A CHAIN

1 **[Fig. 1, red thread]** This is basic St. Petersburg chain. Start by threading a needle on one end of 2 yd. of thread. Leaving an 8-in. tail, pick up four cubes. Go again through the first two cube beads and pull through. **[Fig. 1, blue thread]** Pick up a 15º seed bead and go back through the two cubes you just came out of. Pick up another 15º and go forward through the other two cubes.

2 **[Fig. 2, red thread]** Pick up three cubes, and go forward through the cube your needle came out of and on through the first new bead picked up. Pull through to make a new box of four cubes, which is interlocked with the first box by one bead.

3 **[Fig. 2, blue thread]** Pick up a 15º and go back through the last two cubes exited. Pick up another 15º and go forward through the other two beads in the box.

4 Repeat steps 2 and 3 to the desired chain length. (If you want to count units, count the 15ºs along the upper edge.) End the threads.

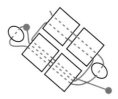

figure 1

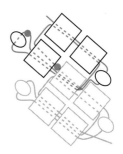

figure 2

CONSTRUCTING THE NECKLACE

Create five chains, each a few inches longer than the previous one. Mine are 10, 12, 14, 16, and 18 in. Attach a closed jump ring to each end of all the chains. Attach one end of each strand to a 1-in. diameter decorative ring, being careful to eliminate any twists in the chains. To wear, place the longest or shortest chain—whichever look you prefer—around your neck, leaving the rest in front. Be sure you have enough length to do this or your necklace won't fit over your head. Another option is to attach separate side chains with a clasp at the back of the neck.

FOR EACH DIAMOND, YOU'LL NEED:

- 4mm cube bead
- 10 1.5 or 1.8mm cubes
- #10 needle
- thread

Single Diamonds for Chain

Make your simple chain sing with a series of brilliant jewel tones or an eye-catching contrast by adding these little diamonds. I placed them between every twelve chain patterns in the necklace. If you're making a bracelet or anklet, you'll want to place them between every nine patterns. You'll be surprised how much wow factor you'll get from this easy addition!

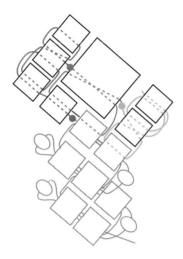

figure 1

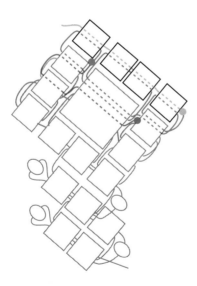

figure 2

MAKING THE SINGLE DIAMOND

1 **[Fig. 1, red thread]** Pick up three small cubes and go through the next-to-last cube again in the same direction. Pull through to lock the two beads side-by-side. Go again through the last bead you picked up in the same direction. Pick up a small cube and go down through the cube you exited.

2 **[Fig. 1, blue thread]** Pick up a large cube and go through two adjacent small cubes on the left. Go back through the large cube.

3 **[Fig. 1, orange thread]** Pick up a small cube and attach it to the fourth cube down on the left of the large cube. Attach another cube to it.

4 **[Fig. 2, red thread]** Go up through the large cube, into the second cube from the right, and back down through the cube on its right.

5 **[Fig. 2, blue thread]** Pick up a small cube and go down through the previous small cube and the large cube. Pick up two small cubes and go down through the large cube and the rightmost cube on the bottom edge. Pick up a small cube and attach it the cube you are coming out of.

6 **[Fig. 2, orange thread]** Go forward through the four cubes on the right edge and pull through.

7 Restart the chain pattern by picking up two small cubes. Go up through the two upper cubes along the right side of the large cube. Pick up a 15° seed bead and go back down through the same two cubes; pick up another 15° and go forward through the two new cubes on the right.

8 To make a chain, follow steps 2 and 3 of the instructions in Chains Necklace, p. 50, and continue the regular pattern, working forward until you have made the desired number of chain units, and then make another diamond unit. Continue making chain and diamond units until you have the desired length, ending with a chain section. Sew a closed jump ring or a clasp onto both ends and end the thread.

Quad Diamonds for Chain

Add even more spice to a simple chain with these expanded versions of the single diamond in which four cubes are held together to make an even larger diamond. Starting the chain, I alternate between units of chain, as in Multiple Chains, p. 50, and single diamonds, as in Chain with Single Diamonds, p. 52. Return to working units of chain and stop after step 3 when you are ready to add a quad diamond.

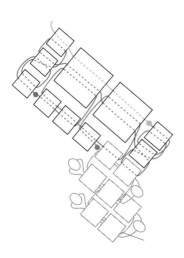

figure 1

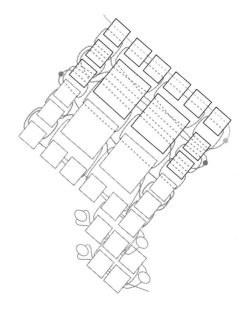

figure 2

MAKING THE QUAD DIAMOND

1 [Fig. 1, red thread] Pick up a small cube and a large cube. Go up through the small cube you just came out of, and go again through the small cube you just picked up. Pick up two small cubes and a large cube, and go through the two small cubes again.

2 [Fig. 1, blue thread] Pick up two small cubes and go again through the first cube you picked up. Go through the second cube again. Pick up another small cube and attach it to the last cube. Continue down through the two large cubes. At the bottom, pick up a small cube and attach it to the adjacent small cube. Pick up another small cube and attach it to the last small cube.

3 [Fig. 1, orange thread] Go up through the two large cubes and the rightmost small cube.

4 [Fig. 2, red thread] Pick up a small cube and attach it to the small cube you just came through. Pick up another small cube and go down through the small cube you just came out of. Pick up a large cube and attach it to the large cube adjacent to it. Pick up another large cube and attach it to the lower large cube adjacent to it. Pick up a small cube and attach it to the rightmost small cube across the bottom. Attach another small cube to that one.

5 [Fig. 2, blue thread] Going through the small cube you just added, continue through both large cubes and the second small cube from the right. Go down through the adjacent small cube to the right. Pick up a small cube. Go down through the cube you just came out of, and continue down through the upper large cube. Pick up two small cubes and go down through the large cube you just came out of and the large cube below it. Pick up two small cubes and go down through the large cube you just came out of and down through the rightmost small cube across the bottom. Pick up a small cube and attach it to the small cube you just came out of.

6 [Fig. 2, orange thread] Continue up through all six small cubes on the right side.

7 To return to the chain, follow step 7 of Single Diamonds for Chain, p. 52, for the transition and then step 2 of the chain instructions for the pattern.

YOU'LL NEED:

- 60 1.5mm cubes
- 16 4mm cubes
- 14 15º seed beads
- ear wire with flat surface
- 2 yd. thread
- 2 #10 needles
- E-6000 glue (optional)

QUAD DIAMOND EARRINGS

1 Leaving a 12-in. tail, make seven units of chain and a quad diamond. Turn the work and using the tail you left, make another quad diamond on the other end of the short chain. End the thread.

2 Attach one of the diamonds to an ear wire that has a flat surface. Some of these come with a double-sided sticky dot for easy attachment, or you can simply glue it with E-6000.

Mirrored Step Bracelet

YOU'LL NEED:

- 3.5g 2mm cube beads in color A
- 3.5g 2mm cubes in color B
- 15–20 center accent beads (optional)
- 30–40 11º seed beads in color A
- 30–40 11ºs in color B
- bar-and-loop clasp
- 4 yd. thread
- 2 #10 beading needles

This bracelet is made using a step stitch variation I call the waltz. This variation alternates a closed and an open section, creating a more lacy look than the basic mirrored chain. You can make this in all one color, but you can also create interest by grouping three beads of one color down the center, as in the two pink bracelets. In the design shown in the instructions, you alternate the colors to create a chevron-shaped stripe. Here, you'll learn how to make the basic two-color bracelet, as well as how to insert a focal bead in the open space. Just do so before you go on to each following section.

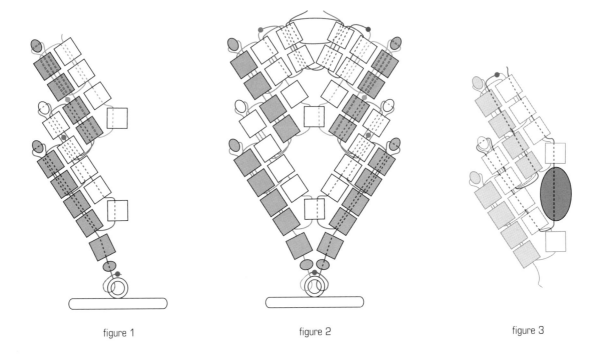

figure 1

figure 2

figure 3

1 Fold 4 yd. of thread in half and attach the folded end to a jump ring or directly to the bar end of the clasp using a lark's head knot. Thread a needle on each thread.

2 **[Fig. 1, red thread]** Starting with either thread, pick up an A 11º seed bead, five A cube beads, and two B cube beads. Go through the fourth and third beads from the needle again to form a box of four cubes. Pick up an A 11º (a turnaround bead) and go back through the four A cubes behind it. ＊ Pick up two B cubes and go forward through the next two B cubes.

3 **[Fig. 1, blue thread]** Pick up a B cube and two A cubes, and go through the fourth and third cubes from the needle (the fourth one will already be in the beadwork). Pick up a B 11º; go back through the two B cubes behind it and forward through the two new A cubes.

4 **[Fig. 1, orange thread]** Pick up two A cubes and two B cubes. Go again through the fourth and third beads from the needle. Pick up an A 11º and go back through the four A cubes behind it. ＊ Pick up two B cubes and go forward through the new B cubes.

5 **[Fig. 2, red thread]** Repeat steps 3 and 4 for the desired length. Repeat steps 2–4 with the other thread, but when you reach the ＊ in steps 2 and 4, go through the adjacent B cube on the first side of the bracelet, pick up one B cube, and go forward through the new B cubes. Repeat steps 3 and 4 to the desired length.

6 **[Fig. 2, purple and green threads]** To finish the bracelet, attach two B cubes to the last two B cubes on both sides, and attach the two new sets of cubes to each other, pulling them firmly together. Sew the loop end of the clasp to the two new pairs, and end the threads.

OPTIONAL CENTER BEAD

7 **[Fig. 3, red thread]** At the end of step 4, turn and go back through the four A cubes adjacent to the row you just came out of, bypassing the 11º. Turn and go forward through the two B cubes adjacent and previous to that row. Go through the 11º at the tip, turn, and go back down through the two B cubes you just came out of plus two more B cubes. Pick up a center bead and go through the next B cube and the three B cubes ahead of it to come out exactly where you started.

8 When you work the other side of the bracelet, repeat step 7 with the other thread, except go through the center bead already in place.

OTHER BEAUTIFUL IDEAS

These three bracelets are made with 1.5mm cubes. The upper version is pink with a grouping of three gold cubes at the center and has no center cubes. I've matched the color of the turnaround beads to the center beads. The second bracelet is the same except a stone bead has been added in the openings. The third bracelet is designed with a chevron stripe and has pearls inserted down the center.

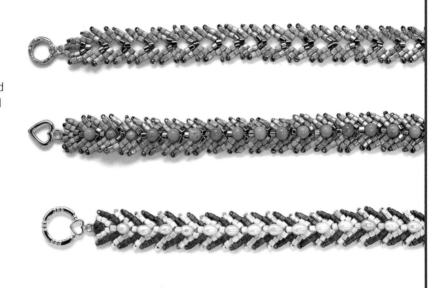

These three bracelets have chevron stripes and are made with 2mm cubes. As above, the upper bracelet is made without any center bead, the second version is made with a center bead. The third bracelet is made with 2mm cubes and 3mm crystal bicones down the center.

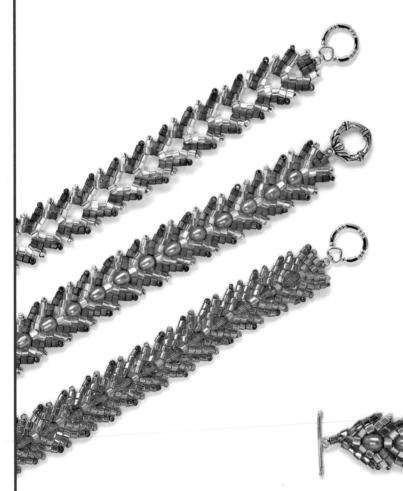

This bracelet is made in the chevron stripe using 3mm cubes with pearls down the center.

Harlequin Bracelet

Harlequin is an old-fashioned name for a buffoon or clown who wore a costume of multicolored patchwork diamonds. This bracelet, with its diamond shapes and many colors, reflects that character. This expanded version of the simple step chain incorporates a Tila bead (a flat, square bead with two holes) between two step stitch boxes. With a bit of inventiveness, you can increase the width of this bracelet. Just add another Tila and box of four cubes (and another set, if you like, for a thick bracelet) at the end of figure 1, and incorporate the width into the remaining steps.

YOU'LL NEED:

- 4g 2mm cube beads
- 25–30 Tila beads
- 40 11º seed beads
- bar-and-loop clasp
- 4 yd. thread
- #10 needle
- 26 drops (optional)

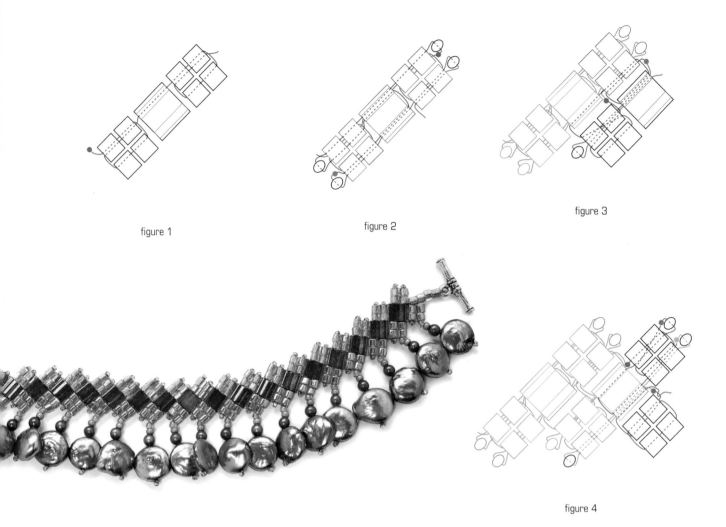

figure 1

figure 2

figure 3

figure 4

1 **[Fig. 1]** Thread a needle on 2 yd. of thread. Leaving a 10-in. tail, pick up four 2mm cube beads, go again through the fourth and third beads from the needle, and pull through to make a box of four cubes. Pick up a Tila bead and four cubes. Make another box of four.

2 **[Fig. 2, red thread]** Pick up an 11º and go down through two cubes, the Tila, and two more cubes. Pick up an 11º, turn, and go up through two cubes and the Tila. Turn and go down through the other Tila hole and the two cubes below it.

3 **[Fig. 2, blue thread]** Pick up an 11º and go up through two cubes, the Tila, and two more cubes. Pick up an 11º and go down through two cubes. (If you are adding drops, do that here.)

4 **[Fig. 3, red thread]** Pattern: Pick up four cubes and make a box. Attach the box to the Tila by going up through the nearest hole in the Tila and continue up through the two cubes on the right of the next box in the previous row. Pick up a Tila and go up through the two adjacent cubes again.

5 **[Fig. 3, blue thread]** Turn and go down through the Tila and the two cubes below. Pick up an 11º and go up through the two cubes and the Tila.

6 **[Fig. 4, red thread]** Make a new box of four cubes. **[Blue thread]** Pick up an 11º, go down through the two cubes and the Tila below it, turn, and go up through the other hole of the Tila and two cubes on the right of the box.

7 **[Fig. 4, orange thread]** Pick up an 11º and go down through the two cubes below it, the Tila, and the two cubes below that. Pick up an 11º (or add drops) and go up through the two cubes and the Tila. You are ready to start another pattern.

8 Repeat steps 4–7 until you have the desired length.

9 **[Fig. 4, purple thread]** To finish, build the next box of four cubes as in the pattern, but stop there and attach half of a clasp between the two inside cubes and the Tila. Turn the bracelet back to the beginning, attach a box of four cubes to the first Tila, attach the other half of the clasp, and end the threads.

Solid Leaf Earrings

With step stitch, it's easy to make a simple little leaf. Combining this leaf with a gorgeous double-drilled crystal bead creates a stunning look. If you've been wondering what to do with some of the new and unusual crystal shapes, this should get you started.

YOU'LL NEED:
- 74 2mm cube beads
- 2 8mm Swarovski double-drilled square crystals
- 30 15⁰ seed beads
- 2 2–3mm closed jump rings
- pair of ear wires
- 2 yd. thread
- 2 #10 needles

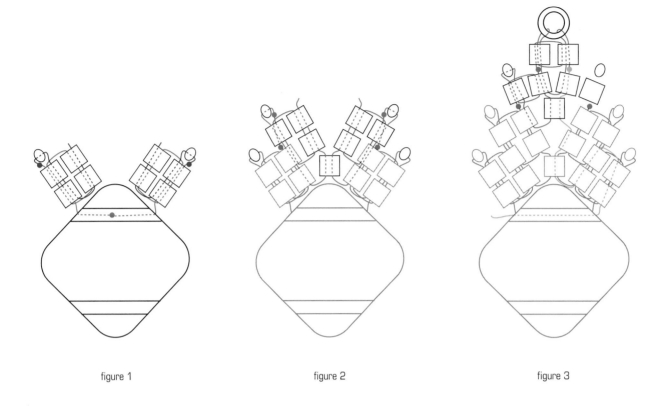

figure 1   figure 2   figure 3

1 **[Fig. 1, red thread]** Attach a needle to each end of 24 in. of thread. Center the thread through one end of the crystal. With one end of the thread, pick up four 2mm cube beads, go again through the fourth and third cubes from the needle, and pull through to form a box of four cubes. Repeat with the other thread.

2 **[Fig. 1, blue thread]** Pick up a 15º seed bead, turn, and go back down through the two cubes below it. Turn and go up through the two adjacent cubes. Repeat with the other thread, being sure your work is centered and your working threads are of equal length. Tighten the boxes against the crystal.

3 **[Fig. 2, red thread]** Pick up three cubes and go again through the upper corner bead of the last box and the first cube you just picked up. Pull through to make an overlapping box. Repeat on the other side.

4 **[Fig. 2, blue thread]** Pick up a 15º and go back down through three cubes. Pick up a center cube and go through the two cubes above it. Repeat on the other side, but go through the center cube you already attached.

5 **[Fig. 3, red thread—shows thread for only one side]** Pick up two cubes, and go through the first cube again to make a half-box. Pick up a 15º and go down through two cubes below it. Pick up a center cube, turn, and go up through the single cube above it. Repeat with the other thread, except go through the existing center cube.

6 **[Fig. 3, blue thread—shows thread for only one side]** Pick up two cubes and go again through the first cube. Pick up a jump ring, turn, and go down through the two cubes below. Turn again and go up through the adjacent two cubes to the right, through the jump ring, and down through the cube you came out of.

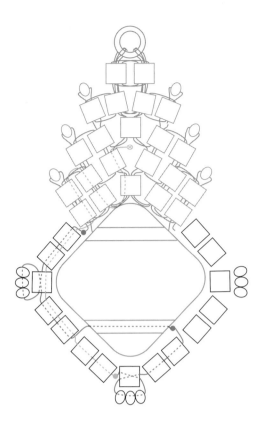

figure 4

7 **[Fig. 3, orange thread—shows thread for only one side]** Follow the path in the illustration down through the work, and finish by crossing through the crystal.

8 With the other thread, follow the same course as the blue and orange threads in **figure 3**. Because the work is symmetrical, you can just turn the work over and repeat. When you finish, your thread will be exiting the crystal in the opposite direction as the other thread.

9 **[Fig. 4, red thread—shows thread for only one side]** With one thread, pick up three cubes and three 15°s. Go again through the last cube. Pick up two more cubes and cross over through the bottom hole of the crystal. Repeat with the other thread.

10 **[Fig. 4, blue thread—shows thread for only one side]** With one thread, pick up three cubes and three 15°s. Go again through the last cube.

11 **[Fig. 4, orange thread—shows thread for only one side]** Pick up two more cubes and, following the illustration, go up through the cubes and into the work above.

12 With the other thread, follow the same course as the blue and orange threads in **figure 4**. Where you meet the first thread, end the threads. Attach an ear wire to finish.

OPTIONAL BOTTOM POINT

To make a point at the bottom, begin where the blue thread begins in **figure 4**. Just turn the earring upside down and make a new leaf as in steps 1–7. Instead of attaching a jump ring, pick up a cube and a 15°, turn, and go back through the cube and continue as in the instructions for the first leaf.

WORKING WITH CRYSTALS

Shaped crystal beads are beautiful, but stitching with crystals is different from using cubes and other seed beads. Here are a few tips for working with them:

Some crystal shapes are solid opaque glass or solid clear glass and don't have a coating. But some beads have a coating, and it can be difficult to tell that it's there.

To see if a crystal has a coating, turn a piece front to back and if you can see a difference, you must decide which side you want to face front. Usually the side without the coating is extemely bright and you can see the holes in sharp definition, while the coated side is darker and deeper in color.

The manufacturers place the coated side toward the back to let the light reflect through the glass and off the coating back to the viewer.

When working with shaped crystal beads, try to keep them protected from scratches. The coated side can wear off, especially around the points and edges of the facets. Keep them in a plastic bag or on a non-scratch surface.

Open Leaf Earrings

The open look of this leaf creates a beautiful shape—almost like wings—which is made using a simple step chain that is joined at the top. The holes of the crystal cube are turned vertically instead of horizontally as in the Solid Leaf Earrings.

These earrings also look stunning if you make them upside down. I've given instructions to do this. I like both versions equally well!

YOU'LL NEED:

- 88 2mm cube beads
- 2 8mm Swarovski double-drilled square crystals
- 68 15º seed beads
- 2 2mm closed jump rings
- pair of ear wires
- 2 yd. thread
- 2 #10 needles

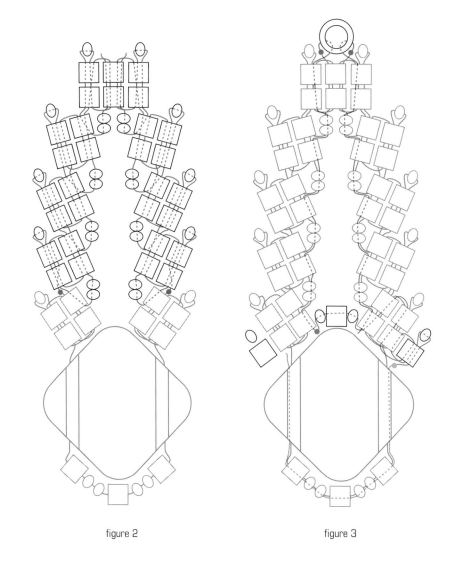

figure 1   figure 2   figure 3

1 **[Fig. 1, red thread]** Thread a needle on each end of 1 yd. of thread. Pick up a 2mm cube, two 15º seed beads, a cube, two 15ºs, and a cube. Take each needle up through one hole of the crystal square and pull through. Center all the beads on the thread so you have equal working threads.

2 **[Fig. 1, blue thread]** With one thread, pick up four cubes, go again through the first two cubes you picked up, and pull through to form a box of four cubes.

3 **[Fig. 1, orange thread]** With the same thread, pick up a 15º, go down through the two cubes below it, turn, and go up through the two adjacent cubes.

4 Repeat steps 2 and 3 with the other thread.

5 **[Fig. 2, red thread]** With one thread, repeat step 2. Pick up a 15º, turn, and go down through the three cubes below it. Pick up two 15ºs and go up through the two adjacent cubes. Repeat this step three more times.

6 **[Fig. 2, red thread]** With the other thread, repeat step 5, except on the last box, pick up only two cubes and go through the adjacent two cubes from the last box on the other side, and then finish the step. Both threads should be coming out of the two center cubes.

7 **[Fig. 3, red thread]** With each thread, pick up a closed jump ring, turn, and go down through the two cubes to the outside of the center and the two 15ºs below it on each respective side. Go through the lower inner corner cube and the two 15ºs below it three times, and then through the final inner corner cube.

NOTE Showing all the thread paths in one illustration gets confusing, so I show only one side for the blue and orange threads in the step below. You will need to make the same pass with the other thread on the other side.

figure 4

UPSIDE-DOWN
OPEN LEAF EARRINGS

1 **[Fig. 4]** Pick up a cube and three 15°s. Pick up a jump ring and go back down through the three 15°s and the cube. With the other thread, pick up three 15°s and go through the jump ring. Go back through the three 15°s and the starting cube. The threads should be exiting opposite sides of the cube. With each thread, pick up two 15°s and a cube, and go through the vertical holes of the crystal square. Follow the instructions, starting with step 2, until you get to the jump ring.

2 **[Fig. 5]** To make the point at the bottom, pick up two cubes and a 15° instead of the jump ring. Go back down through the two cubes and continue as in the instructions. With the other thread, pick up only one cube and use the cube and 15° at the tip to turn around and go back into the work.

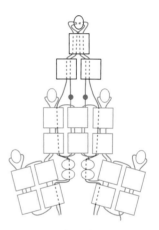

figure 5

8 **[Fig. 3, blue thread—shows only one side]** Pick up a 15°, a cube and a 15°. Cross over to the other side of the leaf. Go up through the two nearest cubes and down through the adjacent two cubes. Pick up a cube and attach it to the cube you just exited. Pick up a 15° and go down through the new cube.

9 **[Fig. 3, orange thread—shows only one side]** To strengthen the thread paths, make another pass down through the crystal square, across through the bottom beads, and back into the work.

10 Repeat steps 8 and 9 with the other thread, but in step 8, go through the 15°, the cube, and the 15° you picked up with the other thread. End the threads.

YOU'LL NEED:

- 86 2mm cube beads
- 4 13 x 7mm Swarovski double-drilled keystone crystals
- 30 15º seed beads
- 2 2mm closed jump rings
- pair of ear wires
- 2 yd. thread
- 2 #10 needles

Crystal Keystone Earrings

I think these are some of the prettiest earrings I've designed, and they came together with a minimum of fuss. Sometimes, things just seem to want to be made! These beauties incorporate a step stitch leaf between two keystone-shaped crystals with a bit more structure to help them hang from the ear wire.

If you've made the Solid Leaf Earrings, p. 61, you'll find that this center shape is similar. You make the center leaf shape, you attach the keystones, and then you add the rest of the construction.

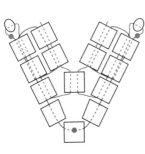

figure 1

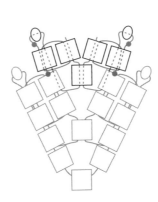

figure 2

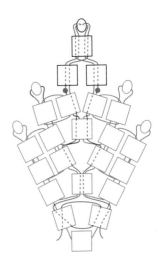

figure 3

1 **[Fig. 1, red thread]** Attach a needle to each end of a 1-yd. length of thread. Center the thread through a single 2mm cube. With one thread, pick up six cubes. Go again through the fourth and third cubes from the needle and pull through to make a box of four cubes. The two cubes that turn back are the "return" beads. Repeat with the other thread, being sure that your thread is centered and you have working threads of equal length on both sides.

2 **[Fig. 1, blue thread]** With one thread, pick up a 15º seed bead, turn, and go back through three cubes. Pick up a center cube and go up through the two return beads. Repeat with the other thread, except instead of picking up a center bead, go through the existing center bead.

3 **[Fig. 2, red thread]** With one thread, pick up two cubes. Go again through the second cube away from the needle and pull through, laying the two beads side-by-side to form a half-box and create a single return bead. Repeat on the other side.

4 **[Fig. 2, blue thread]** With one thread, pick up a 15º, turn, and go down through the two cubes below it. Pick up a center cube and go up through the single return bead. Repeat with the other thread, except go through the existing center bead.

5 **[Fig. 3]** With one thread, pick up two cubes and a 15º. Turn and follow the lefthand red thread in the illustration back to the base. Stop at the last cube before the first center cube and attach it to the adjacent cube on the other side, pulling the two together. With the other thread, pick up a cube and then go through the existing cube and 15º at the tip. Follow the righthand red thread back to the base. Your threads should be coming out of the second cubes from the bottom on the outside, with one cube bead between them.

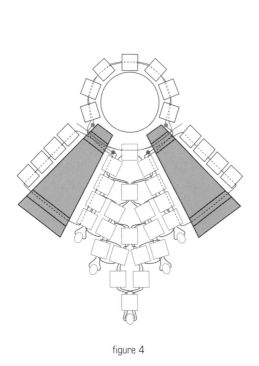

figure 4

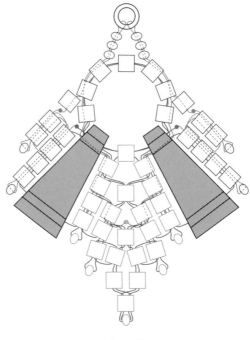

figure 5

ADDING THE KEYSTONES

6 **[Fig. 4, red thread]** Turn the work upside down so it matches **figure 4**. With one thread, go through the short hole of a keystone crystal. Pick up four cubes, go through the long hole of the keystone, go up through the four cubes along the outside of the leaf, and go out again through the short hole of the keystone. Repeat with the other thread and a second keystone. Remember: If your keystones have a different front and back, be sure they are facing the same way.

7 **[Fig. 4, blue thread]** With one thread, pick up seven cubes, and go through the upper hole of the keystone on the other side, the upper center cube, and the upper hole of the remaining keystone. Repeat with the other thread, except go through the same seven new cubes in the opposite direction.

8 **[Fig. 5, red thread]** With one thread, go down through the four cubes along the outside of the keystone, pick up a 15º, turn, and go back up through the same four cubes. Pick up two cubes and attach them to the upper two cubes of the previous four cubes. Pick up a 15º and go up through the two cubes you just added. Repeat on the other side.

9 **[Fig. 5, blue thread]** With one thread, pick up a cube, skip the first cube of the ring, and go up through the next two cubes of the ring. Pick up three 15º's and a jump ring, turn, and go back through the three 15º's, three cubes of the original ring, the short hole of the keystone, and three cubes of the leaf as shown in **figure 5**. Repeat with the other thread, except go through the existing jump ring. Bring the tails together and end the threads.

10 Attach an ear wire to the jump ring. Make another earring, and you are ready to dazzle your friends with this gorgeous design.

This elegant black and silver pair is made using 1.5mm cubes. You'll see that you need five cubes to span the length of the keystone instead of four, and a box of four cubes at the tip instead of two.

Five-pointed Star

This perfect five-pointed star is so versatile! In silver or gold it can decorate anything you choose—from your car mirror to your Christmas tree. Use it as the focal point for a special decorated box or gift. Sew it onto your jeans or jacket for a fashion statement. The tricolor version is hot for the Fourth of July.

The piece uses five short segments of step stitch that radiate around a ring of 11º seed beads. The cube beads lock together at the sides and hold the star shape. The instructions show a single color star, with the red, white, and blue variation included in brackets.

YOU'LL NEED:

Single color
- 5 4mm cube beads
- 3.5g 2mm cubes
- 50 11º seed beads

Tricolor
- 5 4mm cubes, blue
- 2mm cubes, 30 dark blue, 55 silver/white, 75 red
- 11ºs, 15 dark blue, 35 red

Both
- 2 #10 needles
- 2¹/₂ yd. thread
- jump ring (optional)

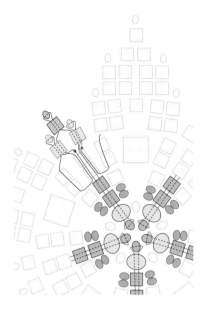

figure 4

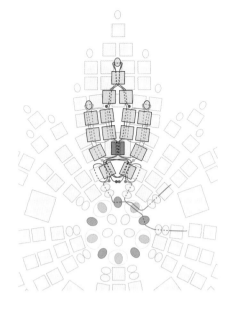

figure 5

MAKE A ROUND OF PETALS ON TOP OF THE STARFLOWER BASE

NOTE The grayed image shows the base star. Notice that the large round beads cover up every other 11º in the original ring. I've colored the original ring of 11ºs blue and made the large beads transparent so you can locate the ring more easily in step 8.

5 [Fig. 5, red and blue threads] Attach the thread by taking each needle out through the beginning cube of each point (they are the ones you picked up after the initial 11ºs). Center the thread. Using beads a lighter shade of the same color as the base, attach a light-colored cube to each of the cubes your thread is coming out of. Then attach the two new cubes to each other with both threads. The action is the same on both sides, but in the illustration I've shown the two sides in different colors so you can distinguish them.

6 [Fig. 5, orange threads] With one thread, pick up five light-colored cubes. Go again through the fourth and third cubes from the needle and pull through to form a box of four cubes. Pick up an 11º and go inward through four cubes. Pick up a dark-colored cube (for an accent) and go out through the two return beads). Repeat on the other side.

7 [Fig. 5, purple thread] Pick up two cubes and an 11º, turn, and go back inward through four light, a dark, and a light cube. On the other side, pick up one cube, go through the existing cube and 11º at the tip, turn, and follow the same path down to the base.

8 [Fig. 5, green threads] To move over to the next base petal and begin another small petal, continue each thread down to the original circle. Go over two beads of the original ring (not the large beads on top of them) and out the two sides of the new petal, coming out in the same position you were when you first added new thread. Continue around until you have made five petals on top of the base star. End the threads.

9 To finish the necklace, attach wires or threads to the closed jump rings you inserted at step 4 and string with matching beads to wear your starflower. If you like, add fringe to the bottom.

TURN THE STAR INTO A STARFLOWER

NOTE Since this is a flower, we will call these points petals.

1 Start with 2½ yd. of thread. Make the single color star (the base) with some exceptions. Start the petals differently: At the beginning of each point, replace the first cube that starts the sides of the point with two 11ºs, and continue to pick up any additional cubes needed to complete the count (see the blue beads in **figure 4**). When you come back down to the original ring, you will go through these two 11º beads, just as you did the cube.

2 [Fig. 4, green beads] When you join the petals, use green 2mm cubes and a matching green 11º to make the two picots. (For placement, see the lighter green beads in **figure 4**).

MAKE THE CENTER CLUSTER

3 [Fig. 4, red thread] Make the first green picot as in step 10 of the original instructions and go down through the four cubes. Instead of picking up an 11º, pick up two cubes, a 3mm round, and an 11º. Turn and go back through the round, the two cubes, and the two return cubes above that.

4 [Fig. 4, blue thread] Make the second green picot, go down through two cubes of the previous point, up through the return beads, and out through the cube of the second picot. Pick up a cube and an 11º. (If you are making a necklace, attach a closed jump ring here and at the next leaf point instead of the 11º.) Turn and go back through the cube you just picked up, the cube of the first picot, and two return beads. End the thread.

Points Collar

This collar has a very pretty, almost lacy look. I like the subtlety of the white and gray combination, which is both neat and a bit sassy at the same time.

The collar consists of a few rows of peyote with step stitch points attached at regular intervals. The white 3mm cubes stand out as accents in the field of matte gray, punctuating the repetition with a little rhythm, while the white 1.5mm cubes provide a plain edge at the neck and an almost frilly edge along the bottom.

YOU'LL NEED:

- 65–70 3mm cubes in color A (white pearl)
- 13g 1.5mm cubes in color B (gray)
- 4g 1.5mm cubes in color A
- 2g 11º seed beads in color A
- clasp
- 6 yd. thread
- #10 needle

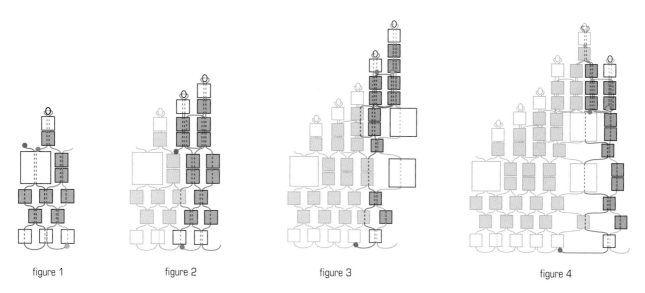

figure 1   figure 2   figure 3   figure 4

Try to keep the tension in each point equal from both sides. Unequal tension will cause the points to skew toward the tenser side.

If your tension loosens, just pull the nearest turnaround bead or the color A cube at the bottom to tighten the previous row, then take the slack out by pulling the working thread taut.

I find it easier to work this piece with the peyote always at the bottom. Since the piece is so narrow, there are only a few steps back and forth.

1 **[Fig. 1, red thread]** Thread a needle on 2 yd. of thread. Pick up a 3mm cube bead, two color B 1.5mm cube beads, and a color A 1.5mm cube bead. Turn, pick up a A, skip the previous A, and go through the next B. Pick up a B, skip a B, and go through the 3mm.

2 **[Fig. 1, blue thread]** Pick up a B, an A, and an 11º seed bead. Turn and go down through the A and B, and pull through. Pick up two Bs, skip the 3mm, and go through the B below it. Pick up a B, skip a B, and go through the bottom A. Turn.

3 **[Fig. 1, orange thread]** Pick up an A, skip an A, and go through a B; pick up a B, skip a B, and go through two Bs.

4 **[Fig. 2, red thread]** Pick up two Bs, an A, and an 11º. Turn and go down through the A and two Bs. Pick up two Bs, skip two Bs, and go through a B. Pick up a B, skip a B, and go through the bottom A. Turn.

5 **[Fig. 2, blue thread]** Pick up an A, skip an A, and go through a B. Pick up a B, skip a B, and go through two Bs. Pick up two Bs and attach them to the adjacent two Bs. Pick up a B, an A, and an 11º. Turn and go down through the A and two Bs. Pick up two Bs, skip two Bs, and go through a B. Pick up a B, skip a B, and go through the bottom A. Turn.

6 **[Fig. 3, red thread]** Pick up an A, skip an A, and go through a B; pick up a B, skip a B, and go through two Bs. Pick up three Bs and attach the last two Bs to the adjacent two Bs. Pick up four

POINTS COLLAR FRONTPIECE

This design also works using 2mm and 4mm cubes. You can make a continuous collar in this size, but it tends to curve faster than the smaller one, so you may get a ruffle effect along the edge. If you want to avoid this, make just a frontpiece and attach beads or a chain to finish the sides and back. Here is how to finish off the ends.

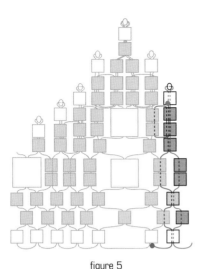

figure 5

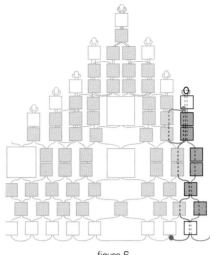

figure 6

Bs, go again through the fourth and third cubes from the needle to form a box, and pull through. Turn the end cubes to the right side.

7 **[Fig. 3, blue thread]** Pick up an A and an 11º. Turn and go back down through the A and two Bs. Turn and go up through the two B return beads.

8 **[Fig. 3, orange thread]** Pick up two Bs, an A, and an 11º. Turn again and go down through an A and four Bs (the two Bs you just picked up and the two newest end cubes). Pick up a 3mm, skip two Bs, and go through a B. Pick up a 3mm, skip two Bs, and go through a B. Pick up a B, skip a B, and go through the bottom A. Turn.

9 **[Fig. 4, red thread]** Pick up an A, skip an A, and go through a B. Pick up a B, skip a B, and go through a 3mm. Pick up a B, skip a B, and go through the second 3mm.

10 **[Fig. 4, blue thread]** Pick up four Bs, go again through the fourth and third cubes from the needle to form a box, and pull through. Turn the return beads to the right side. Pick up a B

and go through the B, A, and 11º of the point already made. Turn and go down through the As and B, plus the two Bs you just added.

11 **[Fig. 4, orange thread]** Turn again and go up through the two Bs you just added. Pick up an A and an 11º. Turn and go down through the A and the two B return beads. Pick up two Bs, skip the 3mm, and go through a B. Pick up two Bs, skip the 3mm, and go through a B. Pick up a B, skip a B, and go through the bottom A. Turn.

12 **[Fig. 5, red thread]** Pick up an A, skip an A, and go through a B. Pick up a B, skip a B and go through two Bs. Pick up three Bs and attach the top two Bs to the adjacent two Bs in the previous row.

13 **[Fig. 5, blue thread]** Pick up an A and an 11º. Turn and go down through the A and three Bs. Pick up two Bs, skip two Bs, and go through a B. Pick up a B, skip a B, and go through the bottom A. Turn.

1 **[Fig.]** Make a short length of points. Starting at the end of Fig. 7, pick up an 11º and a white. Skip the 3mm and go down the next gray. Pick up a gray, skip the next gray, and go down through the bottom white. Turn. Pick up a white, skip the existing white, and go through the gray. Pick up a white and an 11º, turn, and go back down through the white you just picked up. Pick up a white, and go through the white at the bottom. Pick up a white and an 11º. (If you want to attach a closed jump ring to further attach a chain or strand of beads, do it here. Make several passes to strengthen the attachment.) Turn and go down through the white in the second row and the white second from the end of the first row. End the threads.

2 Repeat the finishing on the other end.

3 Make a strand of beads for each side on a doubled thread and sew the tails into the work. Try not to tie any new knots on top of previous knots. You can also attach a chain to each side.

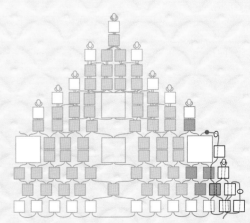

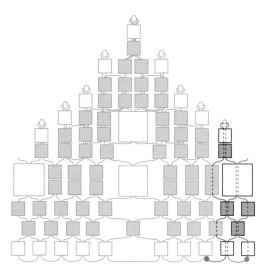

figure 7

14 **[Fig. 6, red thread]** Pick up an A, skip an A, and go through a B. Pick up a B, skip a B, and go through two Bs. Pick up two Bs and attach to the adjacent two Bs.

15 **[Fig. 6, blue thread]** Pick up an A and an 11º, turn, go down through the A and two Bs, and pull through. Pick up two Bs, skip two Bs, and go through a B. Pick up a B, skip a B, and go through the bottom A. Turn.

16 **[Fig. 7, red thread]** Pick up an A, skip an A, and go through a B. Pick up a B, skip a B and go through two Bs. Pick up a B, an A, and an 11º. Turn, go down through the A and the B, and pull through. Pick up a 3mm, skip two Bs, and go through a B. Pick up a B, skip a B, and go through the bottom A. Turn.

17 **[Fig. 7, blue thread]** Pick up an A, skip an A, and go through a B. Pick up a B, skip a B, and go through a 3mm.

18 Return to step 2, **blue thread**, and repeat until you have the desired length. Sew on a clasp, and end the threads.

GALLERY

ASYMMETRICAL NECKLACE
For this piece, I created an off-center look that combines herringbone stitch with strung elements. The strands are accented with pearl, glass, and gemstone drops for a lush look.

RUSSIAN COUNTESS
Make a beautiful necklace using the same stitch as the mirrored step bracelet. This is such a versatile design that I developed nine variations using different colors and varieties of mineral beads. This one features carnelian rounds with 3mm amber glass and gold cubes.

STARFLOWERS
This starflower in navy and light blue incorporates dangles that hang from the joining closed jump rings. This piece uses chain with a sterling clasp to fasten around the neck.

POINTS COLLAR
This collar is made with matte black and gold using 2mm and 4mm cubes. The drops are two different sizes of tortoise shell glass beads.

STARFLOWERS
Three starflowers made with matte ivory 1.5mm cube beads and accented with green are sewn to a peyote band to make a white poinsettia bracelet.

Other Stitches

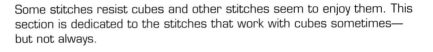

Some stitches resist cubes and other stitches seem to enjoy them. This section is dedicated to the stitches that work with cubes sometimes—but not always.

With peyote stitch, you can get a little play simply by working looser, but you still have to watch what you do with the cubes. The designs I've given you in this section work partly because they are a combination of two or more sizes of beads. This, more than anything else, seems to let the stitch loosen up.

Some of the pieces in this section are a variation of **peyote**. The Three-bead Cuff, p. 81, was a delightful discovery. It incorporates three of the sizes of cubes in a variation of peyote stitch. I also used a peyote-like stitch in the two Tila cuffs, which use two-holed, flat, square Tila beads.

Some pieces made with cube beads tend to become stiff; the sides and the ends lock together, and you have an unmoving piece of work. **Brick stitch** is the biggest culprit, but you can use the stiffness to your advantage to create a solid shape. Locking is tightest when the ends of the cubes are pulled together, as in this stitch. A pyramid is an easy geometric shape you can make with cube beads and brick stitch. It's so rigid you can add fringe for movement.

Basic **square stitch** came in handy when I was experimenting with step stitch, trying to make a diagonal pattern. I used square stitch to extend the box of the step stitch to make a wider bracelet. In the bargain, I got the Diagonal Square Stitch Bracelet, p. 90.

Of course, you can experiment for yourself and find out where these cube beads work for you. I've used them in all sorts of stitches to get one effect or another. You can put them on a loom, just like other seed beads, and you can combine them with round seed beads to create texture and variation. I hope you'll experiment and find many other applications for these remarkable little beads!

Three-bead Cuff

If you have even a little Goth in you, this is your bracelet. It's bold, dark, and has a geometric metallic pattern. I like this version in gray, black, and silver cube beads. For a brighter look, try using blue-brown matte 2mms with metallic dark blue 1.5mms and light gold metallic 3mms as shown in the piece on p. 82.

For a subtle look, choose colors close together. You can go still further and turn this into a multicolor fantasy by using a variety of 3mm bead colors on a background of white or neutral.

YOU'LL NEED:
- **11g 3mm cube beads**
- **12g 2mm cubes**
- **5g 1.5mm cubes**
- **5-ring slide-lock clasp**
- **#10 needle**
- **thread**

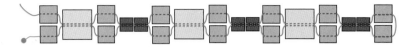

figure 1

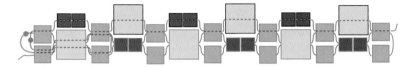

figure 2

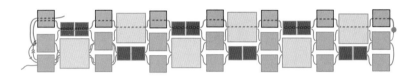

figure 3

NOTE You will have to turn your work after each pass and work in the opposite direction. Since I'm right handed, I turn my work so I'm always going from right to left.

1 **[Fig. 1]** Thread a needle on 2 yd. of thread. Leaving a 12-in. tail, pick up cubes in this order: 2mm, 3mm, 2mm, two 1.5mm, 2mm, 3mm, 2, two 1.5mm, 2mm, 3mm, 2mm, two 1.5mm, 2mm. Turning to the opposite direction, * pick up a 2mm, skip the previous 2mm, and go through the two 1.5mms; pick up a 2mm, skip the 2mm, and go through the 3mm, repeat from * twice, and pick up a 2mm. You have completed the first pass.

2 **[Fig. 2, red thread]** Now you need to turn and make the third pass, but the last 2mm you picked up has nothing to attach to. You will have to make a turn into the work to get in position. Go through the very first 2mm, 3mm, and 2mm you picked up, turn and go through the other 2mm, the same 3mm, and the first 2mm. You are coming out of the first 2mm you picked up; this puts you in position to go through the 2mm that will begin the third pass.

3 **[Fig. 2, blue thread]** Go through the next 2mm, * pick up two 1.5mms, skip the 3mm, and go through the 2mm; pick up a 3mm, skip the two 1.5mms, and go through the 2mm; repeat from the * twice. You are at the end of the third pass.

4 **[Fig. 3]** Pick up a 2mm, skip the 2mm, and go through the 3mm; pick up a 2mm, skip the 2mm, and go through the two 1.5mms. Repeat twice. You are at the end of a pass and need to turn, but again you must attach the end 2mm to something. Because there are an uneven number of beads across, you will have to do this throughout the piece, but only along this side. Catch the thread under the two threads that run between the two

previous 2mms along the outside edge, and pull the new 2mm up against the previous one. Turn, and go back through the new 2mm.

5 Pick up a 3mm, skip the two 1.5mms, and go through the 2mm. Pick up two 1.5mms, skip the 3mm, and go through the 2mm. Repeat twice.

NOTE Be sure you don't pull this side tight, or it will curve and deform your bracelet.

6 Repeat steps 4 and 5. As you progress, just remember that every other row is all 2mms. In the alternate rows, you will switch between the 3mm and the two 1.5mms; if there is a 3mm below, add two 1.5mms, and if there are two 1.5mms below, add a 3mm.

7 End with a row of 2mms. Sew on a clasp, attaching each loop to an end 2mm. End the thread.

Tila Checkered Cuff

This is a bold look when done in high contrast, like the brilliant raspberry cubes against the subtle matte finish of the rainbow Khaki, but the textural qualilty of a single color is also eye-catching. The best match I've found to the size and shape of the Tila beads is a box of nine 1.5mm or 1.8mm cubes. This box matches the Tila bead for both shape and thickness.

The technique used here is basically peyote stitch, but it is necessary to accommodate the two holes in the Tila bead. Consequently, instead of the two passes needed to finish an entire sequence of peyote, you will need three passes. This means you start each sequence on an alternate side of the piece.

YOU'LL NEED:

- 8–9g 1.5mm cube beads
- 8–9g Tila beads
- 5-ring slide-lock clasp
- #10 needle
- 8 yd. thread

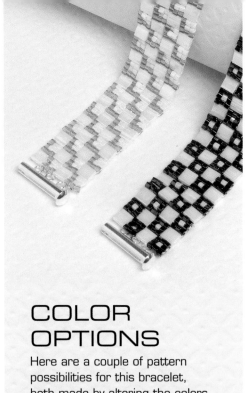

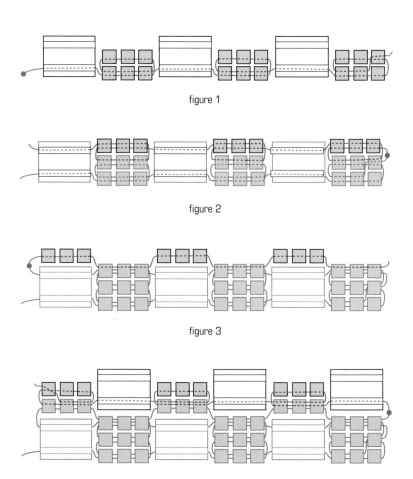

figure 1

figure 2

figure 3

figure 4

COLOR OPTIONS

Here are a couple of pattern possibilities for this bracelet, both made by altering the colors within the box of nine little cubes. In the first one, the two adjacent sides of the box are colored differently. In the second, there is an alternate color placed in the center of the box.

1 **[Fig. 1]** Thread a needle on 1 yd. of thread. Pick up a Tila bead and three 1.5mm cube beads. Pick up another three cubes, go back to the beginning of the first three cubes, and go through them again. Pull through to lay the new cubes against the first cubes. Repeat twice, but in the last repeat, go back through only the first two cubes, and then go through the last cube in the new row.

2 **[Fig. 2]** Turn. Pick up three cubes. Go to the end of the adjacent row of cubes and go through them toward you; that is, backward from the direction you are working. Turn and go through the new cubes again and on through the second hole of the Tila bead. Repeat twice.

3 **[Fig. 3]** This makes the first complete Tila and cube bead pattern. Turn. Pick up three cubes, skip the Tila, and go through three cubes. Repeat twice. This is the first row of the second pattern.

4 **[Fig. 4]** Turn. Pick up a Tila bead, skip the first three cubes in the row below, and go through three cubes. Pick up three cubes, go back to the beginning of the three cubes you just went through, and go through them again. Repeat twice, except in the last repeat, go through only two of the cubes in the row below,

and pull through until the beads are lying side-by-side. Cross over and go through the last cube in the new row. This puts you in the correct position to begin the next row.

5 **[Fig. 2, in reverse]** Repeat step 2.

6 Repeat steps 3–5 until you have the desired length. Attach half of a clasp to each end and end the threads.

NOTE Once you get into the pattern, you will make one pass to lay in the first three-bead row of the box of nine cubes, a second pass to pick up the Tila bead and lay in the second row of the box, and a third pass to lay in the third row of the box and go through the second hole of the Tila. Because you make three passes instead of two and turn every time you make a new part of the pattern, you end up starting a new pattern on alternate sides of the work. Don't let this confuse you. The action is the same. This is a simple repeating pattern, just like peyote.

NOTE The bracelet in the instructions is a cuff six sections wide, but you can work with any even number of sections to make a wider cuff or a narrower bracelet.

Tila Cuff Variation

Like the Tila Checkered Cuff, p. 83, this variation uses the natural combination of Tila beads and cubes for a geometric bracelet. Instead of joining the Tilas with nine cubes, insert five cubes for a striking diagonal effect. I used iridescent shades for my cuff, but it's eye-catching in any other monochromatic color scheme. Try adding a pop of color in the middle cube bead for a completely different look.

YOU'LL NEED:

- **6g 1.5mm cube beads**
- **8–9g Tila beads**
- **5-ring slide lock clasp**
- **#10 needle**
- **8 yd. thread**

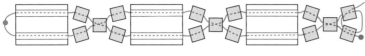

figure 1

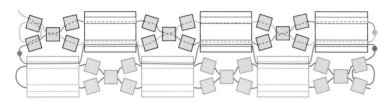

figure 2

1 **[Fig. 1, red thread]** Thread a needle on 1 yd. of thread and pick up three 1.5mm cube beads and a Tila bead three times.

2 **[Fig. 1, blue thread]** Turn and go through the other hole of the last Tila. Pick up a cube, go through the middle cube of the three already there, and pick up another cube. Repeat twice. Go backward through the first cube you picked up and forward through the last cube you picked up. Pull these two together so they are locked side-by-side.

3 **[Fig. 2, red thread]** Pick up a Tila, skip the three cubes, and go through the Tila in the previous row. Repeat twice.

4 **[Fig. 2, blue thread]** Turn. Pick up three cubes. Go through the upper hole of the Tila (the one you haven't gone through yet). Pick up three cubes and go through the lower hole of the next Tila. Pick up three cubes and go through the upper hole of the last Tila.

5 **[Fig. 2, orange thread]** Turn and go through the lower hole of the first Tila. Pick up a cube, go through the middle cube of the three already there, and pick up another cube. Go through the upper hole of the Tila. Pick up a cube, go through the middle cube, and pick up another cube. Go through the lower hole of the Tila. Pick up a cube, go through the middle cube, pick up another cube, and attach it to the cube below it, as in step 2.

6 Repeat steps 3–5 until you reach the desired length, remembering that you are changing directions every other completed row. Attach half of a clasp to each end and end the threads.

Pyramid Earrings

Geometric shapes make absolutely gorgeous earrings. I use 2mm cubes because they make just the right size baubles for me, but you can use 3mms for some super-sized ones, or 1.5mms or 1.8mms for a daintier pair.

These earrings hold their shape because of the flat sides of the cube beads. If you made them with any round bead, they would just roll up. In fact, they are strong enough that you can add elements to them, such as a row of drops along the bottom, fringe, or just a few interesting dangles. If you plan to make fringe part of your design, add another yard of thread to each earring.

YOU'LL NEED:

- 3g 2mm cube beads in color A
- 1.5g 2mm cubes in color B
- 2 3mm closed jump rings
- pair of ear wires or backs
- #10 needle
- 3 yd. thread

figure 1

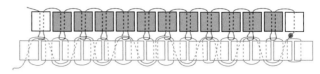

figure 2

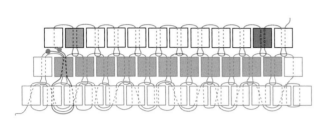

figure 3

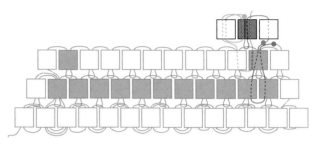

figure 4

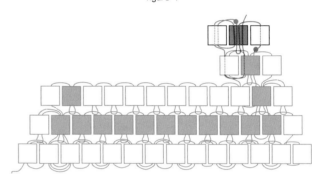

figure 5

NOTE For a fringed version, add 14 fringe beads and 2 yd. thread. Turn your work as needed so you are working comfortably right to left if you are right-handed.

1 **[Fig. 1]** Thread a needle on 1½ yd. of thread. Using a stop bead and leaving an 18-in. tail, build a ladder 14 2mm A cubes wide, but when you attach the last bead, don't go through it again. You will be coming out of the second-from-last cube. Turn the work so the thread points up.

2 **[Fig. 2]** Pick up an A and a B 2mm cube, and attach by passing the needle under the threads between the 12th and 13th cubes of the first row and coming up again through the B. Attach 10 more Bs and one A across. This is the second row.

3 **[Fig. 3, red thread]** To start a third row with a beginning decrease, you need to exit the second bead from the end. To get there, go down through the adjacent B and the A below it and toward the center of the piece, then come up through the adjacent A and out through the second cube in the second row.

4 **[Fig. 3, blue thread]** Turn. Pick up an A and a B, and attach as before. Finish the row with 8 As, a B, and an A.

5 **[Fig. 4, red thread]** Turn as in step 3 to exit the second cube over.

6 **[Fig. 4, blue thread]** Pick up an A and a B and attach between the second and third cubes.

7 **[Fig. 4, orange thread]** Pick up an A and attach with a ladder stitch to the adjacent B. To reinforce the new bead, go down through the cube again and the A below it, turn, and go up through the adjacent cube and into the center cube above. You are ready to make a new short row.

8 **[Fig. 5]** Repeat steps 6 and 7 until you have seven short rows all decreasing toward the center.

9 **[Fig. 6]** Making the second side section: Take up the tail you left and go through the work until you come out the second bead over from the other side in the third row. Turn the work so that you are working in the same direction in which you made the first side. Repeat steps 6 and 7 until you have seven short rows on this side too.

10 **[Fig. 7, red thread]** Choose the longest thread, and make one more row of an A, a B, and an A as in steps 6 and 7, but after you attach the third cube, go down through that cube and the one below it.

11 **[Fig. 7, blue thread]** Attach the cube you are in to the third cube in from the other side. Turn and go up through the cube second over from the right in the row you are in, and in the row above that. Go down through the cube bead over and attach to the threads below.

12 **[Fig. 7, orange thread]** Come up through the same cube, and finish that row with a B and an A. Decrease as in step 3.

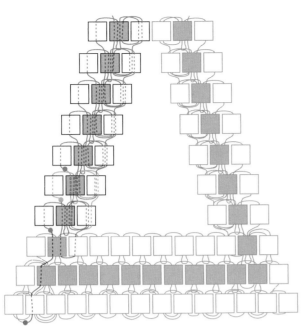

figure 6

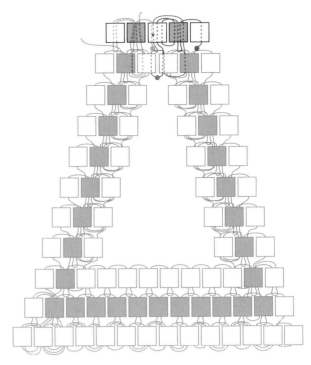

figure 7

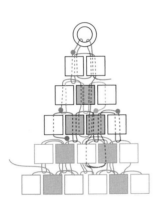

figure 8

13 **[Fig. 8, red thread]** To make the tip, turn and make a row of an A, two Bs, and an A.

14 **[Fig. 8, blue thread]** Work a decrease as in step 3 to get into position for the next row.

15 **[Fig. 8, orange and purple threads]** Make a row of an A, a B, and an A. Decrease again and make a row of 2 As.

16 **[Fig. 8, green thread]** Attach the closed jump ring here by going through the ring and back down through the cube you came out of, over and up through the adjacent cube, and through the ring and back into the cube you came out of. I like to make this pass again, going down through an additional cube below each time to keep the two top cubes from pulling away from the body of the earring. Bring the two ends of thread together in the work and end the threads.

17 Attach an ear wire to complete the earring. Make a second earring to match the first.

FRINGE

To attach a row of drop beads or fringe along the bottom of the pyramid, come out each cube in the bottom row in turn, picking up the drop or fringe as you go. If you are making a graduated fringe and want some control over the shape of it, start at the center bead with a new thread and work your way to each end. I graduated my fringe by two beads each.

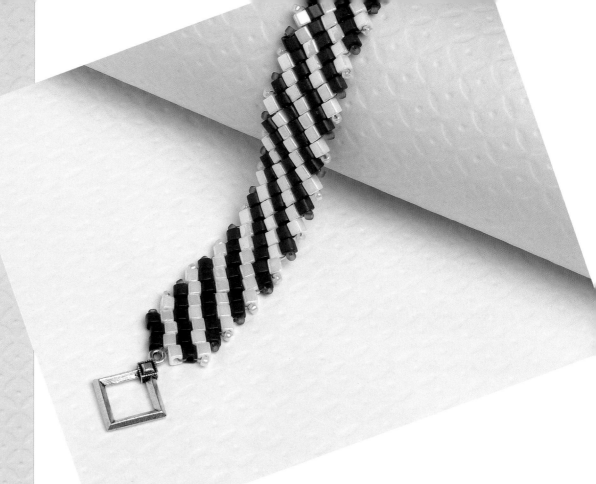

Diagonal Square Stitch Bracelet

This bracelet works up pretty fast using 3mm cubes, but you can also downsize it by switching to 2mm cubes. If you want to make a very fine bracelet or a ring, choose 1.5mm cubes or even little hex cylinders. The hex shape has a flat side that acts like the flat side of a cube to hold the beads in place.

You can add a third color to the diagonal stripe by alternating A-B-A-C, or even use up some of your leftover cubes to make every diagonal stripe a different color for a whole rainbow. The contrasting diagonals seem to attract a lot of attention with accompanying "oohs" and "ahs" and "how did you make that?"

1 **[Fig. 1, red thread]** On 2 yd. of thread, attach a stop bead, leaving a 15-in. tail. Pick up six 3mm A cubes.

2 **[Fig. 1, blue thread]** Pick up a 3mm B cube and go up again through the last A cube. Pick up an A 11º seed bead and go down through two A cubes. * Pick up a B cube and go down through the adjacent A cube plus one more cube. Repeat from the * four times but on the fourth repeat, go down only through the adjacent cube. You will have made a new row of six B cubes.

3 **[Fig. 1, orange thread]** Pick up a B 11º and go up through all six B cubes.

4 **[Fig. 2, red thread]** Pick up a B cube and an A cube, and pull through until the new cubes are against the work. Go up through the B cube again, pulling the two new cubes side-by-side, and take out any slack. Pick up a B 11º and go down through two B cubes.

5 **[Fig. 2, blue thread]** Pick up an A cube and go down through the adjacent B cube plus one. Repeat four times but on the fourth repeat, go down only through the adjacent cube.

6 **[Fig. 2, orange thread]** Pick up an A 11º and go up through all six new A cubes.

7 Repeat steps 2–6. Continue working until you have the desired length. Stop after completing an A row, not including the A 11º. Next you will need to finish off the ends.

8 **[Fig. 3, red thread]** Pick up a B cube, go up through the adjacent A cube and back down through the B cube to lock them against each other. Repeat four times.

9 **[Fig. 3, blue thread]** Pick up a B 11º and go up through four cubes of the B row you just made.

10 **[Fig. 3, orange thread]** Pick up an A cube and attach it to the adjacent B cube, as in the previous row. Repeat twice. Pick up and A 11º and go up through all three A cubes.

11 **[Fig. 3, purple thread]** I like to reinforce the end by looping through the beadwork a few times, and then attaching the clasp to the threads passing between the points made by the last two rows. Attach half of the clasp and end the threads.

12 Fold the bracelet end-to-end and you will see that the beginning looks just like the ending. Repeat the same finishing instructions on this end.

NOTE Remember: When you attach the bar end of the clasp, you need to add enough beads between the bracelet and the bar so it can go through the loop.

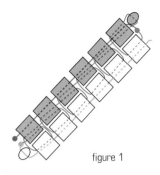

figure 1

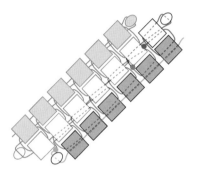

figure 2

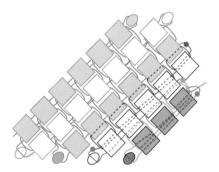

figure 3

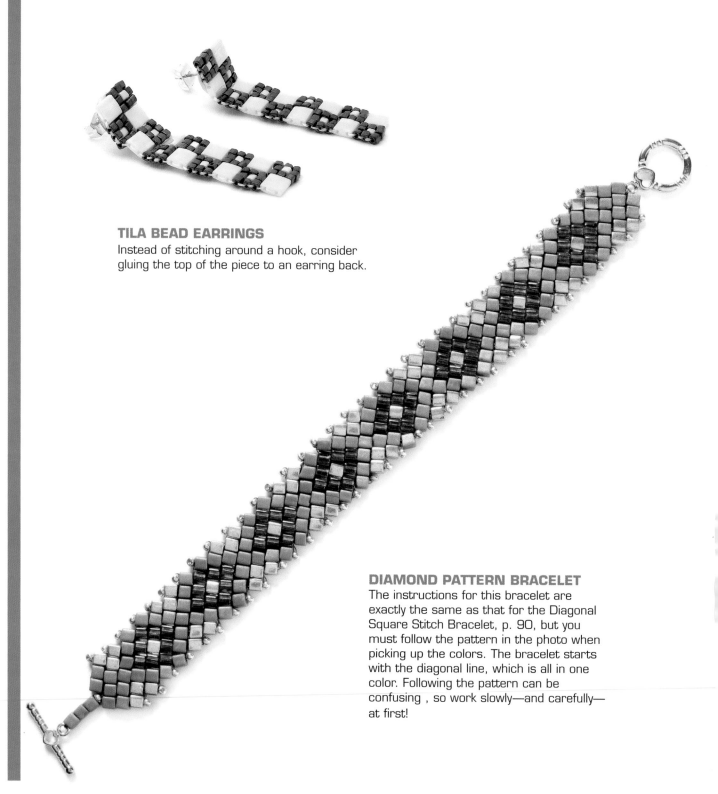

TILA BEAD EARRINGS
Instead of stitching around a hook, consider gluing the top of the piece to an earring back.

DIAMOND PATTERN BRACELET
The instructions for this bracelet are exactly the same as that for the Diagonal Square Stitch Bracelet, p. 90, but you must follow the pattern in the photo when picking up the colors. The bracelet starts with the diagonal line, which is all in one color. Following the pattern can be confusing , so work slowly—and carefully— at first!

Design Thoughts

I don't believe it's necessary to be a wizard at beadwork to create something stylish and wearable. If fact, some of the most popular pieces I've designed have been the simple ones.

THERE ARE A NUMBER OF FACTORS THAT MAKE A PIECE WORK:

COLOR

Your choice of colors and the way you combine them can make or break the usability and fashion sense of the piece. Choose colors that will blend with modern clothing and accessories. Spend a little time looking at the colors in your wardrobe and think about what you would really wear and how well it enhances your overall look.

I like to blend some gold or silver into many of my pieces. People generally favor one or the other and usually have some in their wardrobe. Incorporating an accent of gold or silver in a necklace, for example, will make it work with a pair of gold or silver earrings that you already own. Plus, you won't have the "matchy-matchy" look that's not currently in fashion.

Choosing colors that will be current and still go with your wardrobe can be a challenge. Some people like to put all the colors of the rainbow in a piece so it will go with anything—that's one solution. Another one is to use variations of a single color, say blue, for example. Then your piece is wearable with any shade of blue you have, and even with combinations of blues. Or you can make a piece for a particular outfit and choose colors that enhance it.

In music, some people like a full rich symphony, others a focused clarifying solo, still others a great little jazz or blues combo. Same with the beads.

PROPORTION

Hemlines go up and down. Beads get delicate, then huge. Bracelets go from one, to two, to three, to even five or six inches in width. Pay attention to the current sizes. Currently, oversized chains are "in." We have proportion choices in beads too. I make some delicate 1.5mm cube bracelets for tiny arms, and bold bracelets with 3mm or 4mm cubes for larger ones.

PATTERN

Like proportion, pattern goes through phases. Tiny checks, oversized herringbone, florals as loud as Hawaiian shirts, and bold solid geometrics—this aspect of style is dictated from fashion mavens. But you still have to decide what's right for you.

STYLE

When selecting color, your hair, eyes, and skin tone are part of the color package too. And then the proportion of your own body affects your fashion choices. Are you large, tall, short, or thin? What proportion looks best on you, in spite of the latest fad? This may be even more crucial than current fashion awareness. A tiny bracelet on a large arm makes the arm look larger. A bold necklace on a tiny person makes the person look tinier. If you're short and wear a five-inch cuff, your arm, and your body, will look shorter.

Take a look in the mirror. Look for ways to match and enhance your own size and shape. It will serve you best in the long run.

CLASSIC

The older a style is, the more likely that it gets to be called a classic. A simple string of beads is the most classic and ancient, along with a pendant on a chain. The Egyptians wore collars. The Romans wore hoop earrings. Various types of brooches have been around for ages, since they were used to hold fabric together. The Victorian Era brought in Y necklaces. Flappers were fond of ropes. I believe we are reaching a place in history where we can tap into the styles of any age and wear them at our option.

I've tried to offer a selection of styles in each of my books, so there is something anyone can wear and enjoy. That is really my happiest reward—to have someone make and wear one of my designs.

SOURCES FOR CUBE BEADS

You can talk to your local bead store and see if they will order cube beads for you, and while you're at it, encourage them to carry the line in the store. These are a few sources that I've found online, but if you need something in particular, just search online for "3mm Miyuki cube beads" or "2mm Toho cube beads," for example. Of course vendors are constantly changing their wares, and you might discover other vendors.

BOBBYBEAD.COM, MINNEAPOLIS, 612-879-8181 OR 888-900-2323

Carries 1.5mm, 2mm (only place you can get these retail online), 3mm, and 4mm Toho cube beads; wholesale or retail.

ARTBEADS.COM, 866-715-2323

Carries 1.5mm, 3mm, and 4mm Toho cube beads, and Miyuki 1.8mm cube beads (called square-cut); also a good source for Swarovski crystal beads and Miyuki Tila beads; retail.

FUSIONBEADS.COM, 888-781-3559

Carries 1.5mm, 3mm, and 4mm Toho cubes; retail; also a good source for Swarovski crystal beads and the Miyuki Tila beads.

CARAVANBEADS.NET, 800-230-8941

Carries 1.8mm, 3mm, and 4mm Miyuki cube beads; Tila beads; retail.

LANDOFODDS.COM, 615-292-7001

Carries 1.8mm, 3mm, and 4mm Miyuki cube beads; retail. Also a nice selection of box clasps and slide-lock clasps for cuffs.

ACKNOWLEDGMENTS

I'd like to thank my family for being so supportive and helpful and for encouraging all my beading projects. Thanks also to the excellent editors at Kalmbach, especially Mary Wohlgemuth, who walked me through my first book with the greatest of ease; my new editor, Erica Swanson; and all the friendly, helpful Kalmbach staff.

About the Author

WHAT I'M DOING NOW

It's so good to have finished this book. I'm excited to go on to new things. There is another book in my head about texture and embroidering surfaces that I hope to get started on. And a second book about Egyptian style beadwork. Well, I won't be idle long, I think.

In the meantime I'm doing something in my community that pleases me. I'm participating in a project to bring writing—both prose and poetry—to disadvantaged people in my town. After being trained to teach beginners to write, several of us are going into the community, to pass on the pleasures and benefits of written expression to the homeless, youth in crisis, veterans, and abused women.

I've been thinking about poetry and beadwork. The need for beadwork now arises almost the same way my need to write wells up in me. Sometimes it's a soft urge to share a thought and other times a driving need to express something that just is not easy to say but is real and full in me somehow. That's the poetic urge.

I was reading Jane Hirshfield's book *Women in Praise of the Sacred* and came across the poem below. It was written by the famous Chinese scholar and poet Pan Zhao, a woman who lived in the first century A.D.

How little has changed in the way women understand the world. I handle needles almost every day and recognize their nature. I know the "delicate footsteps" of picking up one bead at a time and incorporating it into something "broad-ranging" under my hand and in my imagination.

The phrase "withdrawing elegantly" calls to mind the quiet place where I work and the feeling I have when other responsibilities have been met and I can focus on those images that have been pestering me to come to life.

How could we calculate the worth of "needle and thread"? Mending, creating, ripping apart and sewing again. While the rest of the world often seems to founder in chaos, these actions tie my days together with a continuity like thread. It's good to be a bead weaver!

NEEDLE AND THREAD

Tempered, annealed, the hard essence of autumn metals
finely forged, subtle, yet perdurable and straight,

By nature penetrating deep yet advancing by inches to
span all things yet stitch them up together,

Only needle-and-thread's delicate footsteps are truly
broad-ranging yet without beginning!

Withdrawing elegantly to mend a loose thread, and
restore to white silk a lamb's-down purity...

How can those who count pennies calculate their worth?
They may carve monuments yet lack all understanding.

(tr. by Richard Mather and Rob Swigart)